The Light Of Rosemary

The First Steps to Self-knowledge

Karina De Oliveira

The light of Rosemary

The First Steps to Self-knowledge

Karina De Oliveira

Sarasota, Florida USA

Contextual Theoretical Collaboration: Aurea Olenka

Cover: Alycia De Oliveira

Final English Revision: Evelyn De Oliveira

Dedication

I dedicate this work with all My love and affection to my daughters Evelyn and Alycia. May this story be an example of success and infinite possibilities in all lessons on the beautiful and funny journey of your lives.

Acknowledgements

Being grateful is a powerful feeling that makes us recognize the small and large joys in life and value the people who make our journey lighter and happier.

So, firstly, I want to thank my dear friend Áurea Olenka, psychologist, who, with her constant enthusiasm, encouraged me to put the ideas in this book on paper. I will be eternally grateful to her not only for her enormous encouragement, but also for her valuable contributions to the theoretical content of this work.

Also here are my most loving thanks to my family: Uilton, my husband; and Alycia and Evelyn (who wrote the preface of this book), my daughters. They were always present with open arms and hearts during my journey of expanding consciousness and mental development. I will always be grateful for the patience they had in working with me during this transformation.

I also want to thank my uncle, the writer Aurélio de Oliveira, a very important person in the development and birth of this book. In fact, I still laugh at his infamous jokes (I can even hear his voice!) said by my character Rosemary. I love you uncle!

Also, all my gratitude to my Divine Self, for placing mentors and important people in my life. Everyone inspired me and helped me see the light of my path. Therefore, here are my thanks to Cristina Cairo, director and founder of the Brazilian School of Body Language and Psychoanalysis Cristina Cairo, to Professor May Andrade, philosopher, writer, mentor, and founder of Temporarily Human and School of Alchemists. Very grateful for your friendship and mentorship.

I also couldn't help but thank teachers Hélio Couto, Wagner Borges among other masters... who left an invaluable legacy of teachings that transport us to other dimensions.

Here is also my deepest and most immense gratitude to my parents Terezinha and Luiz, who have always accompanied me on all my adventures and decisions, many of them full of emotion. I will always be grateful for teaching me to love my daughters. I love you!

Finally, I want to thank everyone who, for space reasons, were not mentioned here, but are no less important. Because, directly or indirectly, they contributed to my success and my growth as a person.

To everyone, I am the result of the trust and strength of each one of you.

Preface

I met Karina nearly 23 years ago in the delivery room when she had me, although, I always felt like I knew her way before that. After living in three different states and two different countries, I can confidently say that we as people are never fully sure of what we are doing, or if we are, we truly do not know if it will go our way or not. We live in a state of patience and trust in ourselves and the world around us, no matter to what degree. I have almost 23 years of experience in this world, four of them spent acquiring a bachelor's in psychology that I use every day...for free. Yet, I learn something that benefits me every day, most of these lessons I learn from Karina, my mother.

When she told me she was writing a book, my immediate reaction was something along the lines of "It's about damn time!" I had no idea what it would be about, only that it was happening, and I was already so proud. Then, she told me it would be in both English and Portuguese, our native language, which excited me even more. What really caught me by surprise was when she asked me to help her and review the English translation of the book. I was both honored and a little shocked to learn she could not think of anyone else to do that, but who else would be better than your own daughter to translate a book.

I sometimes reflect and notice how much credit my parents actually deserve from having the courage to move between two countries not once but twice, the second time with two children. The new environment, language and culture were things we adapted to however difficult it was. As two parents and two children, we had times of arguments and difficulties for the lack of understanding of how we were dealing with the sudden change. Our whole lives, my sister and I were told the privilege it was to have been born in the United States, but neither of us could fully grasp the extent of that until much later.

After one year of being back, we moved to Florida, which brought another wave of "having to deal with it" from all of us, resulting in more heightened emotions and differences of opinions. All of this to say, the mental, emotional, and spiritual journey the four of us went through was completely different, but we did it together.

I like to say that our parents, especially my mother, grew up with my sister and me. As my sister and I went through our teens, my mother went through, what some would call, her midlife crisis. She and I, especially, had our fair share of fights and arguments that would end in a silence that was so loud it hurt. While my sister grew up as the more rebellious child, I was the more confrontational one, which most of the time ended against my will.

The moment my mother decided to start this holistic journey was the moment I knew I needed to change as well. As she studied her way through all of these teachings, I watched from afar taking in all her new ways: the way she spoke, the way she held herself, her confidence in all her beliefs. After some time, I would sit in front of her and ask all the questions that came to mind about what she had learned and her view on all those topics. In all honesty, our friends that met us after this journey would never guess that a couple screaming matches had happened between the two of us.

In our household, we like to say that age is just a number, but my mother seemed younger by the day in this new journey. And, as I got older, we came to be not only mother and daughter but also friends. We laugh and talk for hours about anything and everything this universe has to give.

This book is not one about religious beliefs or views, it is a journey of a change in mindset and positive revelations. It is a manual for those who have always felt there was something missing in their own book of life. Read it, take it in, maybe read it a second time, and understand that it is never too late to change your ways. But most of all, enjoy it! There is no better time to become the best version of YOU than today.

Evelyn De Oliveira
Daughter, Sister, and Friend

TABLE OF CONTENTS

Dedication...4

Acknowledgements 5

Preface 7

CHAPTER 1 The light of Rosemary.....................15

CHAPTER 2 Discovering Therapy.......................22

CHAPTER 3 What do you have in your mind?.....37

CHAPTER 4 Who is the brain?.............................45

CHAPTER 5 Self-sabotage....................................63

CHAPTER 6 "The doctor will find a way!" Caring for the machine 88

CHAPTER 7 Who do you think you are? (Where is your attention now?) 105

CHAPTER 8 Meditation (Every day, I get better and better!) 118

CHAPTER 9 Emotional Intelligence 145

CHAPTER 10 The Pillars of Emotional Intelligence 169

Chapter 11 It was just what was missing!...........181

Epilogue 201

About the Author 203

INTRODUCTION

What is your problem?

Problems... we were born with them!

But look... before we were born, we had no problems! We were just a tiny cell swimming around happily waiting for life to happen. Suddenly, a magical moment! After frantic shaking and, for us, inexplicable groans, we went from bag to sac. Crazy thing! We leave, more like, the paternal scrotum and move into the maternal amniotic sac. We thought this would be a problem.

But it was not! At the time, we were millions and millions wanting, in a mad and desperate race, to reach the prize of life. We didn't know why, but only one would get there. Would that be a problem? We will never know what happened either. We'll never know if we jumped the line or did something tricky with the group... hard to remember! But one of us made it!
Problems with change? No, we had no problems! Actually, it was a wonderful surprise! There were nine months of forming, growth and development, snuggled in the warmth of a welcoming womb, sucking a finger and listening to an anxious mother's heartbeat incessantly. Life was good in there! We had no problems. At least, not that we knew of!

Suddenly, we started having problems! Movement, agitation, shouting and... a slap in the ass! Maybe that was our first big problem: starting life already being beaten!

Yes, it was a first problem that we immediately learned to solve by yelling. Although, later, we would discover that not all problems would be solved like that, yelling!

But it was like that, in that way, that we came into the world and started to live. That's how our problems started. Of course, we weren't yet aware that we had and would have problems from that moment on.
Over the years, we've discovered and learned that problems have always been and always will be part of our lives. Thankfully! Because, if you change the way you see a problem, that is, see it from another angle... let's say, more optimistic, you will see that problems are, in fact, gifts.

Gifts? You would ask... how can a problem be a gift? The best answer to that question lies in the opportunity we gain to face the problem. A chance to have a one-on-one with the problem. No? So yeah... instead of saying gift, let's say challenge!

What is a challenge if not a provocation? A stimulus, that is, that push that you need to go over the problem and see it from the inside and discover all the possibilities to solve it. Once the solution is found, you begin to realize that the problems are no longer actually problems, but challenges.

Challenges are always good. Because it is from facing these challenges. The learning process begins, like an excavator shovel in the immense forest of life, opens its way to important self-knowledge. Because of this, we can say that a problem can also be a gift.

The old Socrates already said: "Know thyself!". He knew things... to know yourself is to know how to modify your relationship with yourself, with others and with the world and, thus, improve and make your journey through life evolve more and more. Socrates, in his legacy, taught us that our life is like a sculpture... in which we go, with the chisel of our attitudes, shaping and perfecting ourselves in the course of our existence.

So, it's about time you looked at your problems differently. It's about time you gave a new definition to that word "problem". From now on, call it a "challenge". Indeed, there are no problems that do not offer a challenge. They always appear, knocking on our door, offering us these challenges. It is good that it is, because, as we have already said, facing these challenges leads us to learning and, consequently, to improvement and self-knowledge.

Benjamin Franklin, great American author, politician, inventor and scientist said that living is facing one problem after another.
Now, the way we face these problems is what makes the difference. And what a difference! Because, if you see the problem as simply a problem, the result is suffering, pain, frustration... but if you see it as a challenge, you will feel the need to face it and, certainly, the result will be your spiritual growth, your evolution. In fact, a problem will always be an opportunity for you to do your best.

In this book, we're going to try to teach you how to be happy with your problems, or rather, with your challenges. Because they will always exist... no matter what size they are. It will always be a challenge, big or small. It doesn't matter!

What will matter and make all the difference will be your ability and wisdom in dealing with these challenges. In this procedure lies your evolution as a person, your self-knowledge and, of course, all your happiness.

So... what are your problems, or rather your challenges for today?

CHAPTER 1

The light of Rosemary

I really like my name... Rosemary! It has a poetic, sublime touch... maybe because it starts with the name of a flower, Rose, which symbolizes everything romantic. Then comes Mary, the holy virgin, a woman who intensely lived her destiny with purity, perfection and, above all, with love! Virtues that inspire us to develop our spirituality.

That's why I've always been very proud of my name. By the way, it is a privilege to have in my ID a name that contains the perfection and poetry of a rose, as well as the virtues of the mother of Jesus. But, even having a name that inspires all this, my life lately has not been like that perfect, poetic nor virtuous. I'll explain:

Have you ever heard of Murphy's Law? No? It's the one that says the following: "If something has the slightest chance of going wrong, it certainly will"! Well, I had one of those days... where not one, but several things went wrong for me. My desire was to find this Murphy guy, stick his head in a can of water and only let go when the bubbles stop.

This day got off to a bad start early in the morning when I had to take a shower with cold water. Just turn on the faucet and the water heater broke. My resistance almost went to space too! I got out of the shower looking like a raisin and went to get dressed. I was already late for my newly acquired job. I decided to follow advice from my grandmother, a wise old lady, who said: "Wear your best panties and the day will be happy!"

Well yes! That day it was as if I had used some of my ex-husband's dirty underwear, who had abandoned me and left a lot of his stuff here at home. Just didn't miss it! By the way, I've never been lucky with men... it can only be that rotten finger of mine that only attracts bad things.

When I arrived at my job, there was a note on my desk. "Pass by HR to settle your accounts". Another one! Well, I'm a telemarketing operator and, probably, I was being fired for having on my first day, mistreated a client like sliced bread: boring, square, thick crust and soft core. I cut the call! Not without first telling him to go where all the bores are sent by those who lose their minds, lose their temper... but don't lose their way home. Well, that's what I did. I didn't even stop by HR (I was only there for two days). I crumpled up the ticket, threw it in the trash and got on my way.

In these hours of anguish and nervousness, the urge to smoke becomes unbearable. I had no money to buy a pack. I only had the money for the bus. Because of this blessed job, I had already given up smoking... I just couldn't remember where!

I went into the house, took off my shoes, my pants, made myself comfortable and went through everything. Somewhere I would find at least a butt! I found everything I didn't need: a hair clip, the TV remote, my nail polish cap... even a lighter!

My salvation was in the little drawer of the bedside table in the bedroom. When I opened it, there he was welcoming me... a Marlboro cigarette more crushed than my resignation note! I grabbed it like an Ethiopian would grab a chicken leg!

I ran to the kitchen, eager to have a cup of coffee and then, yes, smoke the crushed Marlboro. I put the cigarette on the table next to the thermos, hoping there would be some leftover coffee (I had run out of powder). When trying to open the thermos, I found that little misfortune is nonsense.

The lid was jammed and, push from here, push from there... it opened! But it opened with a bang, and I ended up dropping the bottle on the table, spilling the last bit of coffee over my last cigarette.

I felt a kind of vertigo when I saw the totally impractical cigarette, soaked in lukewarm coffee. I even tried unsuccessfully to dry it with a paper towel... nothing! It just fell apart! And so am I... totally pissed off and the cigarette soaked!

Something bad started to rise in my throat, a taste of gall... I don't know! It made me want to cry, but I couldn't even do that. I needed to talk to someone, vent... it even occurred to me to call my aunt. But I put that idea aside. My auntie? No way... having to listen to a whole string of reprimands, destructive criticism, censorship... no! Talking to my aunt was definitely out of the question!

I went back into the bedroom, intending to look in the other nightstand drawer. Maybe there would be another cigarette. Nicotine withdrawal is a bad thing. Look... at that moment if someone offered me a pack of cigarettes in exchange for my mother, I wouldn't think twice "Done deal!" I would say. "Take the runway ex-husband with!"

A nice drag, at that moment, would be like a light at the end of the tunnel. Although, the way I was, the light from the end of the tunnel wouldn't surprise me if it was a train. I rushed into the bedroom and went straight to the other bedside table. Amazing how one bad wave always attracts another. When walking quickly, barefoot, towards the nightstand, in the desperate eagerness to find another cigarette, even a crumpled one, another tragedy!

In the middle of the way there was my bed and, on the bed, there was a leg. Not mine! Mine came soon after, with its blind and unsuspecting little toe. It was there, ladies and gentlemen, it was there, at the corner of the foot of the bed, that I hit and almost took my little finger off! In that millisecond, my brain received the information of what had happened down there and thought: hmmm! This must hurt!

And it hurt! And I let out a roar that would put Mufasa to shame! The pain was increasing, and I felt that my soul had moved a few centimeters out of my body. The pain radiated to other regions: leg, belly, arm... even my ID was hurting. I sat on the bed, holding my little toe, already purple and swollen, and saw myself in the wardrobe mirror. I was disfigured with pain... already half green! I think I was turning into the Hulk...

As the pain increased, so did my ability to curse. I released all the bad words I knew and didn't know, ending with the one in which I praise the maternal entity at the foot of my bed. Shrek would blush...

Limping, I returned to the living room. I needed help. I put on some sweatpants (I had my private area all exposed) and, leaning on a broom upside down, like a cane, I went outside to call my neighbor. Luckily, he came quickly and, seeing me disheveled with a broom, probably thought I was getting ready for Halloween.

I asked him to take me to a medical center and he was an angel. He helped me into the car and took me to the doctor. Then he brought me back to the house and helped me to lie down, with my foot in a cast.

Later, lying on my sofa, in the most complete depression, not knowing what to do with my life... I even thought about suicide! Why not? It's a quick fix... how would it be? Gas? Shot? Throw myself on the overpass? I remembered they cut off the gas! I don't have a revolver either... and where I live there's no overpass! My God what a stage! Not even to kill myself... that's when they knocked on the door.

It was Anita, the wife of my savior neighbor. With a huge scarf covering her head, she came to bring me a warm meal. She told me that with my foot in a cast I wouldn't be able to do anything: "It's not a big deal, but I hope it helps!" Then she told me that she is being treated for cancer and that João, her husband, is unemployed. "Things are difficult for us, but with faith and optimism, we will get there! You too! Have faith and don't let hope die! She also said that they would move to his parents' house where they would have more resources. She straightened the blanket that covered me and left, leaving my heart the size of a pea.

It was at that moment, still lying on my couch, that I managed to cry. Really cry. Of fear. Of regret. Mostly out of embarrassment... cancer? The unemployed husband? And me cursing my life over a cold shower, lack of cigarettes, a lost job and a bruised little toe? And they were even more willing to help me...

I covered my head with the blanket and closed my eyes. Then I saw the light... not that light that takes us upstairs. But the light in the form of clarification, understanding... my neighbors Anita and João showed me that problems are inevitable, and it is difficult for us to stop them. That's when I asked myself: and what is in our control?

With kindness on that sick face, Anita showed me that what's in our control is how we deal with our problems. Even struggling with a bad illness and unemployment, Anita and João were very willing to help me, they were kind to me. They made my problems theirs and had positive attitudes.

With my head still covered and with tears in my eyes, I continued to reflect on those good attitudes and the few words spoken by Anita. Yes, that couple taught me some lessons and the first one is that we must learn to endure our frustrations. But how to do it? Again, that light... we have to assimilate the idea that we can't do everything. What we want is not always possible to accomplish. We must accept life's "no's" and deal with them as if they were challenges and not problems.

Wow... that light was indeed a revelation! Everything became clear to me... in an instant I learned that I must fight for my spiritual growth, for my evolution as a person and as a spirit. I never heard from Anita and João again. In addition to missing them so much, those two left a lesson that I never forgot: to be happy with my problems.

I remembered your suggestion to seek help from someone. But who? A therapist? Who knows...

CHAPTER 2
Discovering Therapy

Reading this far has already shown you that to live is to face problems. They are always arriving at our door, like the electricity bill, water bill and garbage truck. You also saw that the way we deal with these problems, facing them as challenges, is what makes all the difference!

Then you read about that fateful day of mine, when I, Rose Maria, started that day with a forced cold shower. Then I lost my job. Afterwards, I desperately wanted to smoke and, due to this addiction, to top it all off, I broke my little toe. That is, I reached rock bottom... I could even feel the mud on my feet. But later I got to know my neighbors, João and Anita, better. João, who helped me with the pain in my broken toe and Anita, who helped me with the pain of my broken soul.

After 20 days, I took the cast off my foot. Wow... what a relief and what a trauma! I never walked barefoot again. But I found paradise again. I felt motivated, hopeful... so much so that I cleaned my entire house. Because someone once told me or I read somewhere that "a clean and organized home is a balanced mind". That was all I needed at that moment: balance and courage to organize my life. Thank heavens, I managed to get a job selling cosmetics and thus have the money to follow Anita's advice, to see a therapist.

Well, two months later I was already firmly in my new job and already doing therapy sessions. It was another good surprise! I imagined that therapy was just a chat with the therapist. Nothing! The sessions led me to reflect and identify the origins of my suffering and then, yes, from there, with the help of therapy, to find ways to overcome obstacles. I could never have done this alone!

In my first session, my therapist talked about the pain. Both about that kind of pain I felt in my broken toe, and that pain I felt in my soul, when everything seemed to fall apart in my life.

The Pain

Kicking the foot of the bed with your toe really hurts! A hammer to the thumb too! It's moments when you scream all the curse words you know and the ones you don't. That pain you feel on those fateful occasions is physical pain.

But there is another kind of pain: the pain of the soul! This is the kind of pain that will mess with your head, your mind and, consequently, it will mess with your body too. It will end up impacting all areas of a person's life. That's why it's important to take this emotional pain as seriously as you do physical pain. Of course, and look for effective and suitable remedies for healing. This is because pain is an unpleasant sensitive or emotional experience related to an injury, whether physical or psychological. We feel pain when we step out of a zone of stability, or comfort, through some unpleasant occurrence.

"Pain continues to be one of the greatest concerns of Humanity" said PhD Manoel Jacobsen Teixeira – Neurosurgeon at the USP Medical School. Since the time when we lived in caves and ate mammoth meat for lunch, The man has always tried to discover why he sometimes felt pain and what he should do when that happened. Painkillers were still a long way from being invented!

Some graphic records of this remote past of humanity, plus documents written later, prove this prehistoric concern. Today we know, according to Dr Manoel Jacobsen Teixeira, "that the expression of pain varies not only from one individual to another, but also according to different cultures".

Currently, any physical pain can be monitored when something is different in the body. This is because physical pain immediately signals the need to pay more attention to health; or what urgent measures must be taken to remedy some physiological imbalance. However, with regard to psychological pain, it is not always the same.

Emotional Pain

At some point in life, feelings like sadness, anxiety, depression, rejection... are characterized as emotional pain. These are examples of feelings that unbalance a person's psychological and behavioral order.

Consequently, they bring tremendous discomfort, which can trigger negative sensations. In many cases, if there is no proper treatment, it can lead the person to extreme attitudes.

Here are some examples of triggers that can kickstart these feelings:

Loneliness

Those who relate little to other people or who lose important ties throughout their lives can feel lonely. The more a person feels lonely, the more he tends to isolate themselves and create an "environment" conducive to the development of situations of greater emotional imbalance with more physical or non-physical damage.

Low self-esteem

Self-esteem is nothing more than your own opinion of yourself. If you have determination and security in everything you do; if you are fully satisfied with yourself; if you recognize and value your qualities... then your self-esteem is there on the top floor. But, on the contrary, if the opinion you have of yourself is not very good, it is a sign that your self-esteem is on the ground floor. Sign that you are not accepting yourself as you are, have difficulty accepting your own mistakes and fail to recognize your potentials. That they exist, believe me!

Remember: low self-esteem ends up generating a constant threat to emotional health. Those who don't cultivate self-love and don't believe in their own potential tend to inferiorize themselves and sink on their own. Thus, soon there will be room for vulnerability, self-criticism and other negative feelings.

Rejection

Experts are unanimous in stating that rejection is one of the hardest emotional wounds to deal with. Because we don't see them and we can't put a band-aid on! But these wounds settle in our soul and stay there for a long time! This rejection can come from friends, romantic partners, family members, work colleagues... and they didn't always have an intention to reject you.

When feeling rejected by someone, the person will develop bad feelings, which result in questions about their own value and importance. This self-criticism is often unfounded, but it can cause severe emotional pain.

Losses and traumas

There are two types of death: one that we know will happen and another that arrives without prior notice. In both cases, there is trauma from the loss. Especially when the one who is gone will be missed a lot. In the first type, in which death is already expected (someone with a terminal illness, for example), perhaps this trauma does not generate such a deep emotional wound. There will, of course, be sadness and despondency, but an easily healed wound.

In the second case, when death comes like a thief at night, suddenly (a violent accident, a suicide, a disaster...), the trauma caused by the sudden loss is enormous and the emotional wound that ensues is very hard to heal. This is because, when a person goes through a situation like this, in which they lost someone very important, it is very difficult to forget this trauma. That's why these emotional wounds, caused by sudden and irreparable losses, are difficult to heal. But they are curable. Believe me!

Stages of Pain or Grief

Denial

In this first phase of pain, all these emotional turbulences such as loneliness, low self-esteem, rejection, losses, and trauma... bring that desire to cry, lead to despair, liquidate hope and all that the person sees in front of him is a fog gray with uncertainties. The eyes of the soul are clouded in vision and cannot see the light at the end of the tunnel. Result: you almost completely lose your physical strength, the will to move, eat... in short, live! But it is interesting to observe that, despite all this, in this first phase there is a very strong feeling of denial. That is, these turbulences are not taken seriously, and the person desperately seeks to escape this disastrous scenario. Life seems messy and terrible during this phase.

Indignation or Anger

After denial, that is, after frustrated attempts to exempt oneself from emotional problems, the person enters a phase of anger, rage... of indignation! Then, from the depths of the soul, the inevitable questions echo: "Why me? Why always me?" Why? Why? The answers that come from the soul itself are diffusing and confusing, which further increases that feeling of anger with oneself, for going through that absurd situation.

Conformity or Bargaining

If you were asked now what the opposite of courage is, your answer would be...cowardice? It's not wrong... but, in this complicated world of emotional problems, the most appropriate answer would be... conformity or complacency! Because, if the person does not have the courage to face the emotional turmoil of life, they conform. They accept and keep guarding and conserving these ills in the corners of her soul. In fact, most people's philosophy is conformity, and the only reward it offers is that everyone likes you... except yourself!

But the question is: how can you ignore the pain? The suffering? The human being has an easy way out... they have a real talent for making excuses for everything. He always manages to find a way to put hot (or cold) cloths on top of emotional problems. This attitude is one of the main tools of compliance. Pain and suffering become part of the routine and increasingly distance themselves from solutions.

You see... conformity and complacency are bad recipes for your emotional well-being, because conforming or accommodating means giving up. Furthermore, conformity can even camouflage suffering and give you a false sense of relief and an apparent, only apparent, happiness. You know the story that says... on the outside beautiful viola, but on the inside... that's right! So, escape conformity, self-indulgence, and face your suffering. You only overcome yourself when you face this suffering. Not when you run away from it. Think of it like this: living without problems is humanly impossible. That's good... because it is suffering, when seen from this perspective, that builds and elevates us.

Therefore, raise the flag of nonconformity, of dissatisfaction, because in order to be evolving, you must always be dissatisfied and not conformed.

Emptiness and Inability or Depression

Pain and suffering lead us to a state of sadness. This is a fact! That's because sadness is nothing more than the first result of conformity. As we said earlier, conformity leads to a false sense of relief, of apparent happiness. The truth is that pain and suffering have become part of you, of your routine and you then manage to disguise all of it well. For the people around you, you are happy, but inside you are sad. This way you will live, to the point where you are no longer sad because of emotional problems. Yes, you are sad because you conformed, you got used to it... sadness started to be part of your everyday life.

Then, believe me... the days get more boring, nothing makes sense, there is no energy to do anything, nothing is worthwhile. It seems the only thing to do is lie in bed, cover your head and sleep. As if sleep was the only way out, when you can sleep, of course! This is the ideal scenario so that, without you realizing it, a greater evil is installed: depression!

Frustrations

Look... it's impossible for us to go through this life without having our share of frustration. Small or large, frustrations exist and, depending on their size, can lead to the inability to live a happy life. As we said in the previous item, pain and suffering lead us to a state of sadness, to a state of total prostration. Attempts to get rid of this situation, without succeeding, bring us a very strong feeling of frustration.

At this stage, the person struggles to get rid of this sadness. The pain and suffering are not enough, the sadness still comes. It is true that sadness is a natural condition in human beings. But how to get rid of it? After all, we must live and coexist, because there is family, work, friends... well, life is not sad. There are, yes, sad times. At these times, some people tend to appeal, look for more, let's say... exotic support: drugs! The goal is to escape bad feelings, sadness... trying to create good sensations for those hours of sadness.

It starts with licit or "soft" drugs, such as tobacco, alcohol, and medication. But they will never be enough and so they resort to illicit and "harder" drugs. The problem is that it gets worse as the person needs to increase the doses. Quickly, what was just sadness becomes one of those problems. One no... several: anxiety, depression, bitterness, hopelessness, and the worst: chemical dependency!

Pathological Diagnosis

This is the time to seek help! This, fatally, happens when all attempts to ease the suffering are exhausted and it becomes necessary to seek help from a professional in psychopathology. The name is a little scary, but it's not a seven-headed animal (maybe five!) Psychopathology is nothing more than the study of mental and behavioral happenings that affect a person's mental health. Psycho refers to mental or spiritual activities; pathology, on the other hand, analyzes and studies the human body in order to diagnose diseases. It's that simple.

Therefore, psychopathology will analyze and discover the origins of emotional pain and diagnose the degree of suffering and all the harm caused to the person by these emotional abnormalities. But what is "abnormal" and what is pathological? There is a difference to be observed, as each individual has a context, both social and individual. Different. Incidentally, not all abnormal behavior is pathological.

For example: you go to check your lottery game and discover that you forgot to play and that, if you had played, you would have won. There you have it! Immediately, there is an upset, a sadness, the size of the prize you lost. It's a normal, basic reaction after a simple loss. Of course, this varies according to age, gender, culture, and social values. But it's a normal reaction that won't seriously impact your physical state. Unless you bang your head against the wall in anger and get a bump. But then, a little ice will do the trick!

However, you see... the line between normal and pathological is sometimes imperceptible. Therefore, the diagnosis should be made by a qualified professional, either a psychologist or a psychiatrist. Because pathology will treat extreme behaviors, emotions and thoughts that cause suffering that physically impact the person, negatively interfering with their daily life and relationships. These symptoms can certainly indicate the presence of psychological disorders and poor mental health conditions that, of course, require professional intervention. Only through therapy, it is possible to deal with these issues, including better explanations for understanding psychopathology.

Death

Unfortunately, there are cases where the person did not have enough strength to recognize that the world was not against them. They can't overcome their demons, even using all the courage that still remains inside. At that moment, when the suffering becomes unbearable, dark thoughts come to the surface, whose focus is to elaborate the end of one's own existence. Because, for them, death is their last refuge, their last attempt to finally find the peace they dreamed of. Here we are no longer talking about courage or cowardice, but about despair. As if the end of hope was the beginning of death. But this is not the only way out! Life is something very precious and we must never give up on it... even if death is the easiest option.

Pain X Suffering

As has been said, pain becomes suffering for the simple fact that it is not given attention. When this pain is ignored for too long, it becomes suffering. As for pain, healing is much easier, as its definition is immediate and the remedy more effective. Suffering, on the other hand, is more difficult to heal and the recognition process is complicated, as all the pain must be brought to light and, at that moment, the person is tired and rejects all kinds of acceptance of something that was extremely painful.

Now the question that never goes away, especially after all this theory about pain and suffering: How to overcome suffering and avoid pain? Suffering is overcome with enlightenment, awakening of consciousness and self-knowledge. "Cinematic" adventures that Steven Spielberg himself would take to the big screen and everyone else to the therapist couch.

Taking care of emotional health

There is an old Latin saying that goes like this: mens sana in corpore sano (a healthy mind in a healthy body). This is a Latin quote from the Roman poet Decimus Junio Juvenal, who was a big fan of the Greek Pythagoras, who advocated the need to control one's thoughts and maintain the functioning of the body. Pythagoras himself said: "Do not make your body the tomb of your soul".

In fact, physical health demands, every day care such as bathing and brushing teeth, hair, nails, skin care... practicing physical activities and taking food re-education seriously. Including making the living and working environment pleasant. Thus, the same concern must be taken with mental health, taking measures to reach the great objective that is mental and emotional well-being.

Physical or emotional injuries, when simple, can even heal by themselves. It's one thing to hit your toe with a hammer or get pissed off because your team lost the championship on penalties. In the case of the big toe, ice and a few curse words are enough. In the case of your team, "next time we win" and life goes on. But life isn't always that simple... instead of being hammered on the thumb, the person can suffer a heart attack; or instead of losing a championship, one might lose a loved one. Then things get more complicated! These more serious injuries, both physical and emotional, require more appropriate professionals and tools to treat them.

See... if a person feels a little weird and inexplicable pain in the heart, he has to look for a cardiologist. If your tooth hurts after eating an ice cream, you already have to make an appointment with the dentist. Now, if the problem is psychological, they have to look for someone who is qualified to discover the causes of this emotional disorder and apply the most appropriate treatment.

That's why a psychologist, a psychoanalyst or a therapist are the only professionals capable of clarifying any doubts about a possible emotional imbalance. They are the ones who will avoid compromising a quality life and open new paths, illuminating others, and bringing new perspectives and decisions to the temporarily human journey in these different times.

If you are experiencing emotional difficulties, experiencing symptoms of mental illness, or simply want to promote your emotional well-being, therapy can be an effective tool to help you navigate these challenges.

CHAPTER 3

What do you have in your mind?

During a coffee break at one of my therapy sessions, I asked my therapist what fascinated her most about the human body. A few seconds later I realized how much of a silly question I was asking! Of course, for someone in a profession like hers, the only answer, at least the most likely one, would be the brain. But she, with all her patience, gave me an answer quite consistent with her religious convictions and confirming what I didn't know I knew:

___ Rose Maria... ___ she said___ ... when placing Man in this world, God did not play around when he equipped him with a brain, the most complex machine in the Universe. Yes, honey, the brain is the part of the body that fascinates me the most.

I asked her a question as unknowing as I am. How would it be possible to understand the brain? She answered me by remembering a quote from a Norwegian writer, Jostein Gaarder, who said: "If our brain were so simple that we could understand it, we would be so foolish that we would still not understand it."

At first, I was the same! But before I continued asking, she explained to me that it is very common for people to see the heart as being the center of our emotions, when in fact this is a function of the brain. Feelings like fear (wow, my heart was in my throat!); kindness (he has a heart of butter!); pity (It's heartbreaking!); love (My heart beats happily!); and so on!

Actually, all these feelings are produced in the brain. The heart is just a muscle that pumps blood to the rest of the body, including the brain. This, yes, is the center of all our emotions. Very common for people to make this confusion! Our brain, she told me, is the most perfect machine ever created. It's a true gift from God, where we find all the secrets... including happiness! But, like any machine, you need to know how to operate it wisely. It was at that moment that she remembered a dialogue between the Scarecrow and Dorothy, characters from the novel The Wizard of Oz:

___ Look... what I really want... ___ said the Scarecrow___ ... is a brain instead of a heart.

___ But why?___ asked Dorothy.

___ Why, because I don't have a brain... I only have straw!

___ Wouldn't you prefer a heart? ___ insisted the girl.

___ No! I want a brain instead of a heart. Because a fool wouldn't know what to do with a heart if he had one.

___ But listen... ___ asked Dorothy ___ if you don't have a brain yet, how can you talk to me?

___ That I don't know... ___ replied the Scarecrow ___ ... what I do know is that there are many people who seem to have no brains and never stop talking, right?

___ Yeah... I think you're right! ___ replied the girl, frowning and holding her chin!

In fact, my therapist told me, it's not so much the brain that matters in this whole thing. What will really matter is everything that guides you, such as character, generosity, charity, good ideas... in other words, positive feelings. But when the brain is misguided, negative feelings such as fear, frustration, agony, distress, anger and so on arise. Sometimes these feelings can fluctuate between positive and negative, such as surprise and pride.

At this point, I wanted to continue asking questions, but she, excited about this topic, continued to talk about all the complexity of that fantastic organ that is the brain. I found it very interesting...

She explained that for our external world to be well and for us to have a more pleasant life, and for us to develop positive thoughts, our internal world needs to be balanced.

The outer world is the result of the inner world, that is, the psychological is also physiological, as the body physically expresses emotions.

How is your inner world?

At the time I wasn't sure what to answer when she asked me that question. Even so, she gave me some guides, like: listen to your body now and ask yourself: how are you feeling? Talking about emotions with the brain is the same as making it look at itself and verify the chemical relationships that are happening at that moment. For the body and mind to be well, the organism needs to be working in harmony. How do I achieve this? I asked. Simple... watching food, sleep, physical activities and so on.

All of this directly affects the brain, which is responsible for giving commands to all other organs. But never forget, she said, that the brain is influenced by thoughts. The brain, like a supercomputer, is programmable. If you program the computer with the concept that 2 + 2 equals 5, what do you think it will answer when asked what 2 + 2 is?

It will answer wrong... 5. Because that's how it was programmed! So is the brain, which must be well programmed with good thoughts so that it always receives good influences.

Your brain, honey, is an organ that weighs about three pounds and has about 86 billion neurons, which are specialized cells for transmitting nerve impulses. But to function properly, it needs energy. Therefore, daily, he consumes about 500 calories. In fact, 20% of all the oxygen you breathe is just for it. Well, nobody works for free, I thought.

The brain, housed within the cranial box, is divided by a very narrow opening in length. This opening is known as the *longitudinal fissure*, which divides the brain into two parts called a hemisphere, therefore two hemispheres.

North and South? I asked, giving indisputable proof of my complete ignorance of the brain. She laughed and explained to me that North and South are the hemispheres of the planet.

Oh, yeah, okay! But what about the brain? What are these hemispheres? I asked. She, of course, with the utmost patience explained to me that many people think of the brain as a single mass. However, when examined more closely, it can be seen that there is a long, narrow opening dividing the brain into two halves. This opening is the longitudinal fissure I told you about earlier, and these two halves are known as the hemispheres of the brain.

Scientists long ago discovered that the right hemisphere controls the left side of the body and the left hemisphere controls the right side. But you see, these two hemispheres of the brain are separate, but they are not completely independent of each other. They are connected and are always exchanging ideas with each other.

She also explained that within each hemisphere are smaller sections known as lobes, which are small lobes of the brain. Lobes? That's right, she replied. Look, Rose, everything you are, everything you think... is there inside that fascinating and complex organ, the brain, an indisputable proof of our success as a constantly evolving species.

Incidentally, the cerebral lobes constitute the four major areas (frontal, parietal, temporal and occipital) of the brain. These lobes always work in harmony, and it is in them that our conscience is installed; it is because of them that we have a language, a memory... it is with them that we regulate our emotions, in short, they are the ones that cause countless other processes. These cerebral lobes are actually divisions of the cerebral cortex, which is a kind of outer layer that covers the two hemispheres.

You know, Rose Maria... explaining the brain, with all its details of anatomy, structure, functions, would take a long time because it is a very complex organ. Volumes and volumes have already been written about it, because the brain is more, much more, than a simple accumulation of neurons. Even this comparison I made just now of the brain with a supercomputer is too small to reflect the brain's full size.

I told her that, as such, the brain beats any supercomputer. She, laughing, agreed with me, and explained that, technically speaking, to better understand the brain, it is important to know that each of the cerebral hemispheres controls one side of the body, the exact opposite of each side of the hemispheres.

For example, that little toe I stubbed on my left foot at the foot of the bed... so, the pain impulses created by the nerves in my little toe were sent to the right side of my brain.

Well, Rose, she completed... in short because, as I said, this topic is so complex that I don't want to put a knot in your brain. See this little set up:

Central Nervous System - made up of the brain and spinal cord.

Main Parts - Inside the skull, it has three main organs: the cerebrum, the cerebellum, and the brainstem.

Brain – we've talked a lot about it. Inside the Nervous System Central, it is the most important and is divided into two parts: left hemisphere and right hemisphere.

Cerebral cortex – is the outermost layer of the brain, responsible for thinking, seeing, hearing, touching, tasting, speaking, writing, etc. It is also the area of memory, reasoning, intelligence and imagination. It also controls the voluntary movements of the body.

Cerebellum – this is behind and below the cerebrum... it is the one that coordinates the precise body movements and helps us maintain balance. It also regulates the degree of contraction of muscles at rest.

Brainstem – lies at the bottom of the brain and conducts impulses nerves from the brain to the spinal cord and vice versa. Breathing movements, heartbeat and reflexes like coughing, sneezing, and swallowing is up to him.

Spinal cord – is a nervous tissue that lies within the spinal column. At the top, the spinal cord is connected to the brainstem. It conducts nerve impulses rest of the body to the brain and coordinates the involuntary acts, that is, reflexes.

In our next session, Rose Maria, we're going to talk more about the brain. Let's go a little deeper into how you work, about its performance as a true mega computer inside our body and its importance for the proper functioning of our organism. Are you up for it?

Okay, I replied, curious and looking forward to the next session.

CHAPTER 4

Who is the brain?

When I responded to Dr. Norma, my therapist, that I was willing to continue with this topic, I thought she was just talking the talk. Because, considering everything she said about the brain, I thought she had already exhausted the subject. Yes! It even seems like gossip from a Mexican soap opera... it never ends! Look, honestly? Good thing, because the subject "brain" just got even more interesting!

I asked her how the brain, doing everything it does, with all the capacity it has... where does it get the energy for all this? Yes, because a car to work, it has to use gasoline; a computer must be plugged in; If you want to cook lunch and dinner, you have to have gas in the cylinder, right? And the brain...what is its "fuel"?

Look Rose Maria, she replied, you must remember what I already said about this. The best fuels for the brain are a balanced diet, a good night's sleep, physical activity... and so on. But, just like the car and the stove, where we need to save gasoline and gas... the brain also needs to save energy to maintain good functioning. Because his work is incessant. Lasts 24 hours a day!

I was thinking... without the right to paid weekly rest? Good grief.

Rosemary, the polymath

Well, Rose... she continued... of all the organs in the human body, the brain and heart are probably the ones that work the hardest and never have a single break! Do you know Aristotle? The great philosopher and polymath of ancient Greece? So... about the brain he said the following: There is nothing in our intelligence that does not pass through our senses. He said this very appropriately, especially because he had a privileged brain.

Would you like some tea, Rose? she said, filling her own cup and, before I said yes, she also poured a cup for me. I took advantage of the pause to ask a question that kept nagging at me. Doctor Norma... I asked... is a polymath someone who works with polishing?

With the cup close to her lips, taking a sip of tea, she sprinkled tea everywhere in a futile attempt to laugh with her mouth closed. Then she burst into a hearty laugh. Moments later she recovered herself and resumed her professional pose, but not before wiping away a tear. Still half serious and half laughing, she exclaimed:

Oh, Rose... you caught me off guard! Now I can't imagine Aristotle other than polishing something... and she laughed again and again! Well, I said without knowing I was making a joke... maybe polishing statues and columns, which was what they had most in ancient Greece, right?

Again, she laughed, nonstop! She returned the cup to the coffee table, placed her hand on her chest and resisted a little the urge to continue laughing. I, a little embarrassed (I didn't know I was a comedian!) was half laughing, half serious. For me, a polymath is a guy who works with polishing, whatever it is... statues, columns, nails... isn't that what a polymath does?

No, dear... she explained, now composed, but still giggling... a polymath is a person who knows a lot, who has knowledge not just of one area, but of many areas. In other words, Aristotle was a polymath because he had great knowledge about everything.

Oh, okay.... I replied... a little frustrated, because I was already thinking about opening a nail salon, specializing in nail polishing. I even imagined a luminous sign outside with the text: ROSE MARIA, POLYMATH... your nails shining like you!

But Rose... she said, cutting off my thoughts... I was talking about Aristotle's phrase. So, repeating what he said: There is nothing in our intelligence that does not pass through our senses. In fact, Rose, everything, absolutely everything you see, hear, smell, taste or touch... everything is processed immediately by the brain. He absorbs everything, separates the information he deems most important, making it more accessible. The most irrelevant, unimportant information is sent to the unconscious.

For example, when you leave the house to go to work or to the supermarket. You look at everything along the way, you hear every noise, you smell smells, perhaps of a bakery baking bread... all of this is irrelevant. Surely, when you're home again, you won't remember any of these details. This is because the brain records and processes everything that your five senses detect, but does not preserve this information because it is irrelevant to you. It will only preserve the most important ones, that is, those that stir your emotions or catch your attention for some compelling reason.

Imagine Rose that, on your way home from work, you witness a terrible accident. From the horrible sound of braking, the dull and tragic sound of the car hitting someone's body... people screaming and running, the body lying on the asphalt, blood... anyway, everything you saw will be fixed in your memory. Because it is a striking fact, and the brain immediately registers it as relevant information. When you get home, the images of the accident will certainly still be fresh in your memory and will remain there for a long time. Very different from the smell of bread from the bakery that, of course, ended up in the unconscious.

My goodness, doctor, if I see something like that... I don't think I'll even sleep at night!

Normal, Rose... all the most shocking facts that happen in our daily lives are marked in our memory. Precisely because they are shocking, striking. Why don't we forget the people who are dear to us after they die? Because they were relevant in our lives. The brain knows this! But it doesn't have to be the death of a relative! For example... she said, looking at the ceiling trying to remember something... who was the Brazilian Formula 1 champion who tragically died in a race?

Ah, Airton Senna... wow, I cried so much! And I wasn't even a fan of racing... poor thing!

Well then, Rose... this is a fact that will never leave your memory. In fact, in the memory of all Brazilians. Just as the attack on the twin towers in 2001 will never leave the memory of Americans. Just say "nine eleven" to any American, and all those horrible images will come to light immediately. This is because the brain, as it is a relevant event, always leaves this information available. Remarkable events remain fixed in our memory!

Will they stay forever, doctor? I asked, remembering important events in my life, such as my separation from that punk, the loss of my job, my broken little toe, etc... Yes, Rose Maria, forever... but over time they lose their emotional intensity, but they will always remain in our memory. But only the striking facts... irrelevant details of our daily lives go to the archive. Maybe you would ask me... how does the brain do this? How does he know what's striking and what's not? Well, it is based on our senses... your reactions to what you see, hear, touch, feel... is what will tell the brain whether it is remarkable or not.

But doctor... I interrupted again... I'm imagining a 70, 80-year-old person, who has lived to the fullest, seen a lot of things, witnessed many events... how can the brain register and process all of this? Even because we only use 10% of it, right?

No Rose Maria, it's not true... forget about this 10% thing once and for all. This is complete nonsense created by who knows! All people use 100% of their brain. What we don't use are our capabilities that can be developed. At least 100% of them! Either because they don't know how, or because they are too lazy to, for example, read or do crosswords, practice intellectual activities... to just focus on these examples. But there are a series of initiatives that help us develop the ability to think and reason.

But you asked me about the brain's storage capacity. See, Rose... like I said, he only keeps the most relevant facts. Unimportant details go into the unconscious and will be forgotten there. This happens because the brain needs to save space on our storage and thus not become overloaded. In fact, the brain's capacity to make this storage goes beyond the biggest supercomputer! Your capacity is infinite! So much so that a person, who lives to be 90 or 100 years old, may very well remember important facts from their youth. Because the brain, as they are relevant facts, has preserved this information, making it available for the person to access whenever they want.

But I'm not just talking about remarkable facts linked to tragedies, deaths of relatives, etc. I also talk about some daily habits that we have, whose procedures are as if ingrained in our memory. This is precisely what scholars call the brain's "autopilot".

Sometimes, Rose, I go into the bank to get some money. I go to the ATM, open my bag, take out my wallet, take out my card, insert it into the machine, type in the password and the amount. I remove the card, the money and put everything in my wallet. I leave the bank and, a few minutes later, I get a scare. Did I take the card out of the machine? Did I put it away? I open my purse again, my wallet and go check. Thank God the card is there.

How many times has this happened to me, girl! Do you know what happens? While I was in the moon thinking about the fact that I needed some money, my brain, after I entered the bank, practically opened my purse, my wallet, took out my card, inserted it into the machine, entered my password... and the value, of course, I decided when I came to my consciousness. But the rest... it was all on autopilot.

Many things we do on the brain's autopilot, without needing to consciously dedicate ourselves to the task. Driving, for example: trivial things like accelerating, changing gear, turning the signal... these are actions that don't require much of your attention. The same also happens with emotions and emotional reactions. In other words, in daily habits... everything that becomes commonplace becomes automated for the brain. Examples like these exist aplenty and illustrate our "autopilot", that is, the brain's ability to perform repetitive mechanical tasks without us needing to pay attention to them.

So, Rose, monitoring your thoughts becomes challenging, precisely because of this theory of automation. That's why it's difficult for us to change an ingrained habit. Because the brain literally fights to maintain what is already known to it. For a depressed person, for example, having depressed thoughts is a habit. Therefore, this person is unlikely to have positive thinking in the face of adversity.

Let's explain this better. Rose... what is a habit? Would you know how to answer?

Well... I answered a little hesitantly... either it's the habit of always doing the same thing or it's a nun's outfit, Father. Or is it both... I don't know! I think that's it...

You're not so wrong, Rose... she said condescendingly... in fact, a habit is a kind of routine behavior. Just like a habit, it is also a religious garment. Wearing a habit is putting on Christ. But the habit, say the ancients, does not make the monk, although there are controversies. But let's get to what really interests us!

As I already said, a habit is a routine behavior, that is, a constant way of performing a certain task. Each person has their own habits, although some habits are common to everyone. For example, brushing your teeth is a common habit for everyone, but there are those who prefer to brush as soon as they get up in the morning; and there are those who prefer to brush after having breakfast.

I prefer to brush as soon as I get up... I said, interrupting... to get rid of that mummy breath!

Well then, Rose... she said without laughing this time... you share this habit with millions of people. But there are millions of other people who only brush their teeth after breakfast. The important thing is to know that there are good habits and bad habits and both are shared by millions and millions of people.

I understand... I said... but doctor, how can we change or stop a bad habit? I, for example, have a smoking habit. Which is not good, right?

Terrible! she replied, frowning and closing her eyes in a kind of silent rebuke. Smoking is extremely harmful to the brain, as it causes serious damage to the cerebral arteries, compromising the irrigation system.

After that, I even lost the desire to smoke a little bit!

Breaking a habit, Rose, whatever it may be, is generally more difficult than creating another habit. This is because these bad habits are always reinforced by continuous practice and also by physiological factors, such as cigarette addiction, for example, which creates chemical dependency. Sugar also comes into this account or chemical narcotics. The truth is that the consumption of these products has strong links with dopamine, a neurotransmitter associated with the feeling of well-being.

But doctor, I asked... without wanting to interrupt and already interrupting: how can I get rid of a bad habit? Is there a recipe for that?

Yes, she replied, but the main ingredient is willpower. Look Rose... the more we fight against a thought or a desire, the more we want to do the opposite. For example, you as a smoker... suddenly, after a small impulse of common sense, you say: "I'm going to stop smoking!". Immediately the brain, accustomed to this habit, hears: "I think I'm going to light one more!" And, that's it, there goes the willpower!

Studies indicate that a good way to convince the brain to change a bad habit into a good habit is to create a new habit, a good one of course, to replace the old one. It's better than repressing your brain! You can, for example, swap cigarettes for gum. But know that this change does not happen overnight. The brain is not that fickle! This is because the brain immediately understands that gum is not nicotine and will not produce the sensation of pleasure brought by nicotine. The important thing is to maintain the strongest motivation to quit the addiction once and for all.

Acetylcholine	This was the first neurotransmitter to be discovered. It is important for muscle stimulation; for the functioning of the autonomic nervous system; It is also important to regulate sleep; and in cognitive functions such as memory and learning.
Dopamine	It acts on different regions of the brain. Its function is to influence our emotions, learning, mood and attention. It also acts by controlling the motor system. In fact, lack thereof can affect movements.
Serotonin	This neurotransmitter acts throughout the organism... from emotions to motor skills. It helps with blood clotting, bowel movements, bone well-being, prevents nausea, regulates good mood, also regulates sleep, helps people relax and is a stimulant of sexual appetite.

Noradrenaline	This is the "fight or flight" neurotransmitter. When faced with any type of stress, such as fright, surprises or strong emotions, it triggers some reactions such as: narrowing of blood vessels, faster breathing, enlargement of pupils and acceleration of heartbeat. But it also contributes to pleasure, concentration, excitement physical and mental, good mood...
Oxytocin	This is the neurotransmitter of love! It regulates social interactions, the expression of emotions and libido, increasing pleasure in the most intimate contacts. In men, it reduces aggressiveness, favors ejaculation, and regulates prostate growth. In women, it facilitates childbirth and breastfeeding.
Endorphin	Neurotransmitter hormone that provides well-being and pleasure. It allows the person to have psychological improvements, slows down aging, improves the immune system, creates physical and mental disposition and resistance.
Adrenaline	This is the neurotransmitter of strong emotions! In moments of great excitement, it stimulates the heart, increases blood flow, accelerates breathing, dilates the pupils when in the dark, increases sweating, increases blood pressure and much more!

Research indicates that an ingrained habit takes an average of 66 days to change. But this is not accurate. It might take more, it might take less. It always depends on the person's willpower.

Oh, doctor... can I give up smoking? I mean, I already dropped it... I just don't remember where!

Rose, dear, she told me without paying attention to my lame joke... see: sleeping more, exercising regularly and even adopting relaxation techniques such as meditation are among the measures you can take to increase your willpower and your brain health.

Doctor... just now you mentioned neuro transmitter... what exactly is a neurotransmitter?

Neurotransmitters

Neurotransmitters are responsible for the functioning of the brain and all body functions such as speaking, walking, eating, sensations of cold, heat, pain... all are controlled by synaptic transmissions (communications between neurons). They are known as the body's chemical messengers, as they are molecules used by the nervous system to transmit messages between neurons or from neurons to muscles.

Many neurotransmitters are built from amino acids, while others are more complex molecules. Currently, more than 100 neurotransmitters are known. Below are some of the best known by people, for their important functions in the body, such as: dopamine, acetylcholine, glutamate, and serotonin. Let's see each one of them, Rose...

For all these neurotransmitters to flow naturally, you just need to have good habits that promote the proper functioning of the brain, understand Rose?

I understood, Dr. Norma, I replied, now I understand why the brain is inside a bone box, the skull. It needs to be well protected, right?

True Rose, you observed well, in this aspect nature was very wise in surrounding the brain with such protection. But, in addition, the brain needs more care from its owner, to function well and without problems.

The brain needs care.

You see, Rose, when we store our memories, we are establishing constant connections. This also protects our brain from premature aging. That's why it's essential to practice physical activity, eat correctly and deal well with our emotions.

Look doctor, I interrupted saying... maybe I'm not taking good care of my brain. As for physical activity, the most I do is get up in the morning; eating I eat everything, I have no filter for food. As for emotions, it's best not to comment...

Rose, she said, just stopping smoking is a big step forward! Understand... all our experiences, everything we live is stored in our brain, which is made up of neurons and cells. He is like a machine full of gears. Therefore, living a healthy life and introducing new knowledge every day lubricates these gears, making this machine work better and better.

We all have a lifestyle that can sometimes lead to illnesses that could have been avoided. Stress, high blood pressure, bad cholesterol, obesity... all of this can be avoided and controlled. These are problems that can inevitably lead to anything from a simple headache, caused by a stressful day, to even neurovascular accidents.

So, dear, taking care of our brain is fundamental, through good eating and behavioral habits, which will make our gray matter enjoy a good state, preventing or delaying some diseases.

Bad lifestyle habits such as poor diet, exposure to radiation and chemical agents (pesticides), sedentary lifestyle, use of chemical substances (cigarettes, alcohol) terribly affect the brain and influence our mood. Depression often arises because the person certainly did not take such care, that is, they did not take proper care of their brain.

Neuroscientists, doctors and beloved therapists offer advice that our ancestors, indirectly, have always passed down from generation to generation. Rose... I'm going to give you some examples of how to take good care of your brain. Look:

HEALTHY EATING

Avoid excessive use of sugar or salt, do not consume transgenic (modified) foods, avoid highly processed foods. Eat lots of fruits, vegetables… and proteins in the ideal amount for your weight and height. Avoid caffeine consumption after noon. This is because caffeine blocks neural receptors, preventing the brain from realizing that you are tired. Be extra careful with stimulants other than caffeine, such as energy drinks that contain a lot of sugar.

RESTORATIVE SLEEP

Sleep is that period in which the body uses it to recharge its batteries and cleanse the brain, as this is when body activity is much lower. Sleeping the necessary hours, seven to eight hours a day, regulates and balances the body and its activities without overloading the brain.

This will keep cells healthy and prepared for their perfect performance. Avoid exposure to artificial light at night. Slow down at least 2 to 3 hours before going to sleep. Consuming caffeine after noon, even if you think there is no difference (at least for some people), directly affects the quality of sleep. For some, it increases anxiety and racing thoughts when trying to sleep.

Caffeine, also used in the production of medicines, has a half-life (the time it takes for a medicinal substance to leave half of the body's composition). This half-life varies from organism to organism, and may take 4, 6 or more hours to leave the organism.

This means that, even if you don't realize it, the caffeine will be there affecting the functioning of the brain. Diseases such as low immunity, obesity, diabetes, heart disease, Alzheimer's, cancer are very likely to develop when the necessary hours of sleep are not met.

MOVE YOURSELF!

Practicing physical exercise, in addition to positively affecting your entire body, helps relieve stress, promotes improved blood circulation and oxygenation, increases the release of serotonin and endorphins and prevents neurodegenerative diseases. With exercise, the body sends more oxygen to the brain, increasing the number of synapses. Rose, did you know that the most effective long-term remedy for anxiety is physical exercise?

I didn't know, doctor... I replied... now, if I have a little money left over at the end of the month, I'll join a gym.

Rose... if you can't go to a gym, do something that's free. Take walks... 45 minutes three times a week. And you can do it in two installments... 20 in the morning and 25 in the afternoon.

HYDRATION

This may seem very complex, but the truth is that it is not difficult to take good care of your brain. If you want to be able to remember things easily, drink water. According to the World Health Organization – WHO – an adult man weighing 60kg should drink at least 2.5 liters of water per day. You may have a balanced diet, but if you don't consume the necessary amount of water, your brain will not reach maximum performance.

THINK CAREFULLY!

Thoughts also feed the brain! Imagine you are watching a horror movie. You know it's not really happening or it's a good thing it's not happening to you. Now, you know that this is a movie, with actors, sets and technical crew. Even so, your brain reacts as if it were true, discharging adrenaline into your body, preparing you for fight or flight.

When I watched Anabelle, I interrupted, my brain only knew how to prepare to flight because, for the fight... not me.

Oh! Oh! Ah!... laughed Dr. Norma... Rose, I admire your sense of humor. This is good for the brain, you know? But I've seen that this humor disappears when you watch a horror film. You feel tremors, sometimes you even sweat, you feel scared, you want to cover your eyes, run away, you feel anxiety... everything as if the scene were real! This happens because our brain does not distinguish the stimuli you send to it as being true or false. He just reacts!

Now think of someone who is having an anxiety attack. How does this happen? It all starts with a series of thoughts and, suddenly, the entire organism reacts with an extreme symptomatic picture, often similar to a heart attack. By controlling your thoughts through breathing techniques, in most cases you can get out of the crisis. (This requires training and guidance/psychological/therapeutic care). With this we see that thoughts directly affect the way the brain will react and give coordinates to the entire organism.

So, Rose... don't forget! It is your daily habits that will directly impact your brain health. It controls the entire organism... therefore, it is essential to maintain healthier habits and, little by little, lose bad habits, which are only harmful to the brain!

CHAPTER 5

Self-sabotage

It's been a while since I was in Dr. Norma's office, when we sat there talking for over an hour. She told me everything about my brain... how much I have to take care of it by creating good habits in my daily life and eliminating bad ones, etc. Right! Easier said than done!

I try... I swear I try. But it seems that there is something stronger than me, which is driving me to continue with bad habits. I keep smoking, I keep eating wrong at the wrong time, I go to bed late, and I can never get up in the morning with joy in my heart. On the contrary... I wake up in the morning in a mood that would scare the Hulk. In fact, this bad mood starts with having to get up. I like to stay asleep until late... then yes, take a nice shower and go out in the mood to sell my cosmetics.

Well, I actually have a lot of willingness to sell, since I need to make money to survive. The problem is that it's difficult to find people with the willingness and money to buy! Yes! Nobody wants to buy anything! Not a deodorant, not a bottle of nail polish, not a lipstick... oh, the sleaziest bunch, I believe, and without vanity! This makes it difficult to secure food in the fridge... speaking of the refrigerator, lately I open it exclaiming: Holy Moly... oly... oly...oly... there's nothing! thing... thing... thing... that's right... my fridge is already echoing! And what's worse... it looks like a poor vegetarian's fridge... whenever I open it, it's potatoes... and that's it!

I have been seriously thinking, for some time now, about changing jobs, a permanent job that guarantees me a salary every month. But what about the courage to change? To start looking... I keep putting it off! Leaving it for later! It's the same when I want to stop smoking... "I'll start on Monday"! Monday arrives and there I am smoking like crazy, with a grumpy face.

But looking for and finding a good job is more difficult than quitting smoking. Looking for a job involves calling, talking to people, opening a newspaper, and looking at the classifieds. I even do that... circle the most promising ones with a pen, cut them all out and put them in my bag. Monday I'll go after it! I'm definitely going! I go with my head held high, with the air of someone who wants to conquer the world! Then Monday comes... did you go? Yup! Me either! Where's the courage? So, I keep putting it off, putting it off... and then here I am in my kitchen, smoking and cooking some potatoes! And now... who can help me? Yes, not even Chapolin Colorado...

I even thought about asking her for some advice, Dr. Norma, an accomplished, well-rounded woman... wow, I want to be like her so much! That's when the idea of asking her for a job occurred to me. Wow... why not? I could serve her clients, offer them tea, a magazine, while they wait their turn... talk to them, in fact I'm good at talking, I look good... what? Am I well dressed? It would make her clinic the biggest success! It's decided! Early on Monday I go to her and... look! Here I am again with this Monday story! Monday, I do it, Monday I go, Monday I start... enough! Let's resolve this problem right now! Where's my cell phone?

Hello? Dr. Norma? It's me, Rose... how are you? Great! (...) Me? Oh! I'm going... eating out of the can, sleeping in the little house... you know, that dog's life! Oh! Oh! Oh! Just kidding, doctor... don't get me wrong... (...) huh? Cigarette? Oh, doctor, unfortunately I still belong to that despicable race that are smokers... but, after our conversation, I'm smoking much less and coughing with less force! (...) Yes, I know, I know... smoking less won't solve anything, right? (...) It's true, it's true... smoking less would be like instead of jumping from the 30th floor, jumping from the 15th... right? (...) Oh! Oh! Oh! I like it when you laugh at the nonsense, I say... (...) it's true, laughter is the best medicine! (...) Come again? Oh yes, I continue to sell cosmetics, but it is difficult, women are more willing to spend money at the butcher's than on beauty! A little steak in your stomach is more important than a little nail polish! (...) True? Are you vegetarian? Wow, that's a good customer! (...) No, doctor, I'm not. I've even thought about being a vegetarian, but when I remember that there are carnivorous plants, I immediately change my mind! In fact, our ancestors wouldn't have invented bows and arrows to hunt cabbages, right? Hello?

Doctor? Hello? (she is laughing) Oh, hi Doctor Norma... I'm here... huh? Stop by the office? But that's exactly why I'm calling... I'd like to make you an offer! (...) Yes, a proposal... I have a great product to offer you! (...) Come again? No, it's not exactly a sale, but I'd like to talk in person and... (...) what product? Well, what a product... when we meet, I'll explain... (...) that's right then... agreed!

Two days later, as agreed, I was ready to go to Dr. Norma's office. After the shower, I fixed my look, wore discreet makeup, put on a boyfriend outfit... and before leaving I took one last look in the mirror. Wow! I would propose to me... and there I went!

As always, Dr. Norma welcomed me with her eternal welcoming smile, a kind of business card! She is a beautiful woman, already in her... maybe... 45 years old? Perhaps! But with a youth that would make Disney princesses jealous. Velvety skin, perfect teeth, hair that was not white, but gray... a bluish gray, which gave her an aristocratic first lady look. But happily married...

Come in, Rose, please... she told me with surprise and kindness... wow, you look beautiful! I missed you... of having a good laugh! But sit down... would you like some tea? So... what do you have for me? What's the news? You told me on the phone that you had a product to show me, although, without wanting to discourage you, I'm not very fond of cosmetics. I like what is natural. My ex-husband... may God rest his soul... used to say that many women are beautiful during the day. But at night, after a shower, all this beauty runs down the drain with soap and water. I believe that the best cosmetics a woman can wear are a smile, charm, elegance... that makes any woman more beautiful!

Wow... I never thought of that! I never thought I was a saleswoman of artificial beauty! But I only agreed with the doctor until page 3... I think that many women need to feel beautiful and, some, only with the help of cosmetics. A little lipstick, some mascara... I don't know! They help a lot!

I also didn't imagine that Dr. Norma was a widow... so young! Well, I wasn't that lucky! That piece of shit of my ex-husband must still be bothering someone's life out there! I thought it best not to discuss this matter with her, after all I was there to ask for a job. Not to talk about ex-husbands or to sell cosmetics. I thought I'd get straight to the point!

It's true, doctor... I said... you really don't need any cosmetics. In fact, you using cosmetics would be the same as putting a string quartet on a rap concert (she laughed). But I didn't come here to show you the products I sell, but rather one product in particular.

What do you mean, Rose? she asked, looking at me, frowning and showing a slight smile, showing friendly curiosity. What product is this?

I picked up the cup of tea and took a sip and, still holding the cup at face height, (I thought that was charming!) I replied with a silly little smile: You're looking at it!

Tea??? Are you selling tea? she told me, eyes widening... I almost fell off the chair. But I didn't lose the pose... Nooooo, doctor... I exclaimed with a discreet laugh. I returned the cup to the coffee table and opened my arms: Me, doctor, I am the product...

I don't understand, Rose... explain this story to me properly! she said, sipping some of her tea. From the expression on her face, serious and questioning, I felt that she had, perhaps, already realized my intention. It seemed to me that, at that moment, a curtain was closing and, like a sparrow fleeing in fright from the presence of a cat, I saw my job flapping away. I decided that truth and sincerity are like dry, red wine... a little bitter, but they fit in any glass.

Doctor Norma... I started, measuring my words... the truth is this...

Then I told her the whole story of my discouragement and lack of courage to do things that are important to me. I talked about my habit of putting things off, leaving everything for a Monday that never arrives. I told her everything! Until the moment I had the idea of asking her for a job, which would be a permanent job and such. I talked about the total dedication I would have to the office, my availability, that I would have a time to come in but not a time to leave, etc... etc...

Rose... she began with some gravity... we'll talk about employing you here at the office later. First, I want to tell you about something that I think is most important at the moment. You see... postponing, leaving something for later, in the sense of prioritizing other things, may even be normal behavior.

But when this starts to become common, commonplace... it's a sign that you've lost track of what's a priority or not. So, I can assure you that this is extremely harmful to you.

Is it a disease, doctor? I was already asking, worried. Because I... No! she cut... but it's a bad habit that has to be replaced by a good habit because, over time, this bad habit can generate a disease or problems in the body. In psychology we call this "procrastinating." Procrastination can be linked to several factors... mainly anxiety and low self-esteem. It is the first of the saboteurs that compromise your personal development.

So, doctor... I said, interrupting... does that mean I'm a procrastinator? It even seems like a serious religious sin! I'm already seeing myself in the Last Judgment and an angel, wielding a sword of fire, points at me and shouts at me: "You procrastinated! You're going to hell!" Then, of course, I'm going to tell this angel that… "that's right! I'm going Monday!"

Calm down, Rose… she said laughing… no one goes to hell for procrastinating. In fact, anyone who lives procrastinating as if it were an addiction already lives in a kind of private hell. See, Rose… procrastinating means postponing something or prolonging a situation. It means delaying, that is, leaving important matters to be resolved later.

But why does this happen, Dr. Norma… I asked… why do we leave things that are important for later, for Monday…?

Well, Rose… the causes can be psychological or even physiological. Psychologically speaking, procrastination may have to do with anxiety and self-esteem issues. You, for example, when you think about stopping smoking… you certainly know that cigarettes are bad for you. But, on the other hand, you also know that, if you don't smoke, you will feel irritable, you will have insomnia, you will be anxious, restless… smoking makes you feel comfortable, right?

Did she have to remember this damned thing? I thought, my throat itching.

Probably, already thinking about these problems, you will not stop smoking. Because you don't want to leave that comfort. Now, Rose, physiologically speaking, procrastination has to do with the brain, more precisely with one of its most interesting areas: the prefrontal cortex. This region of the brain concerns the planning of behaviors, especially the more complex ones, and also has to do with the expression of personality. To give you an idea of the importance of the prefrontal cortex, Rose... it is responsible, among other things, for controlling impulses and determining focus. Do you understand dear? she asked... I understand, Dr. Norma! I responded without much conviction...

For me... I thought... cortex is more like a condom brand! Doesn't it match? But I didn't say anything...not me. I had to be smart... especially because my cortex was already distracting me from the doctor's explanations, and I needed this job! I took a sip of tea and crossed my legs holding my chin with my right hand and gave my number 42 gaze, which means deep interest and job speculation.

Do you know what I think is happening, my friend? she asked, making a note on a pad. You are self-sabotaging!

How so? I thought, looking away, already frowning and giving a new look, the number... I don't know what number, but which presupposed fright and concern. Would I have become a terrorist of myself?

She noticed my reaction and tried to reassure me. Rose, she said... self-sabotage is when you, consciously or unconsciously, place difficulties and obstacles in the things you have to do. In fact, it is negative thoughts and feelings that lead you to engage in self-destructive behavior.

Is this procrastinating? I asked, feeling uncomfortable about it. Exactly, dear, she replied... procrastination is perhaps one of your main saboteurs. But let's understand this better. Let's go back to talking about how our brain works, especially when it comes to our habits and how this procrastination thing can interfere with the development of new and good habits.

At this point I had even forgotten about my job... self-sabotage? Me, terrorist?

You see, Rose... she said, interrupting my thoughts... everything that is automatic saves time and energy, right? This way the brain will always try to automate everything possible. We already talked about this, remember? I gave you the example of driving a car... after you get in it, you close the door, turn the key in the ignition, look in the mirrors, put it in 1st gear and get out. You've gained some speed, you shift into 2nd gear, increase speed further, shift into 3rd gear and so on. Along the way, if necessary, you honk the horn, turn on the left or right turn signal, turn on the radio, give a light signal. If it starts to rain, you turn on the windshield wipers... all this, Rose, you do without the slightest thought. Because the brain has already automated everything for you!

I understand, doctor... I said, terrified of her asking me if I knew how to drive. The only thing I've driven so far, and badly, is the supermarket cart. But I maintained the pose, returning to my gaze 42...

I mean Rose... she continued... that driving is just a Rose example among thousands of other more important ones. In other words, everything you do without the need to reason is because it is already part of your habits. Your brain has probably already automated this for you. In fact... this is one of the reasons why breaking an old habit becomes so challenging!

I wanted to ask her what Rose meant, but I kept to myself! I thought it would be embarrassing to show ignorance. To me, Rose looks more like church tiles. I thought... *the Our Lady of Help church is covered inside with colorful* Rose... I was laughing inside but, on the outside, I kept my gaze 42: Wow, that's interesting, doctor!

Rose, dear... certainly you, not always consciously, stop doing something, procrastinating, precisely to stay in your comfort zone. In other words, continue with old habits because they do not require physical or mental effort. I'm sure you sometimes light up a cigarette even if you don't feel like smoking.

Here she comes with the cigarette story again! The want to light one! I understand doctor...I said with that 42 gaze.

Well then, it's the brain's automatic pilot working, leading you to smoke because that moment, and not your body, asked for a cigarette. It's such a psychological addiction! But there are also other more complex aspects that involve procrastination, such as low self-esteem, doubts, anxiety, etc. By the way, Rose... procrastination, as a habit, causes stress, a feeling of guilt, leaves you unproductive and then, dear, this can bring illnesses to the body.

And where does self-sabotage come in? I asked, still thinking about terrorizing myself.

See Rose... she replied... everything that is already known generates more comfort. On the other hand, every change generates discomfort. The inner desire to escape is almost natural for people who believe that living well is living without any kind of discomfort. Procrastination creates obstacles to evolution, change and creates space for a cycle of self-sabotage.

So, you're saying, doctor... I asked... that when I postpone or leave things that I have to do until later, I am self-sabotaging?

That's right, consciously, or unconsciously, you are refusing to change and leave your comfort. You are putting yourself against yourself, demotivating yourself and not believing in your potential. Out of fear, you miss opportunities that could contribute positively to your life. And what's worse...you kind of self-sabotage yourself almost without realizing it.

How to identify self-sabotage

But Dr. Norma... I asked... if I practice self-sabotage without realizing it, how do I know I'm self-sabotaging?

Good question... she said, pouring more tea... do you want some too? Look Rose... she replied, filling my cup with more tea... procrastination is one of the ways to self-sabotage. It's not believing in your own ability to solve problems or finish a task. Then procrastination begins, that is, leaving activities and responsibilities for later...

Keep putting it off, keep putting it off... I said, adding and taking a sip of tea... that's right Rose, keep inventing excuses to constantly postpone pending issues and not have to deal with them. If you don't try, you'll never get out of this, and the feeling of failure will increase.

Precisely for this reason, dear... that changing a habit ingrained in you can be very challenging... not to mention very difficult! But not impossible, let's be clear!

Rose, I'm going to ask you some questions, but you don't need to answer me. Just think about the answers, okay?

I nodded "yes" and always kept my gaze 42, but I was already afraid... what kind of question was she going to ask? Well, whatever it is... I'm glad I just have to think.

These are simple questions... she told me... but the answers, I believe, are more complex in your head. So just think about these answers. Let's go? First... how is your life? What are my main habits? How are your results? Are you where you want to be? What goals do you want to achieve? Think about these questions while I make a call and I'll be right back. Make yourself comfortable... have more tea!

Thank you, doctor... I replied, pouring myself more tea while she left in a hurry carrying her cell phone. I kept thinking about possible answers to these questions... how is my life? It hasn't been walking lately, but it's been lazily moving! My main habits? After this tea all I think about is smoking. What results is she referring to? I don't have any positives... just the blood! Even the raffle ticket I bought from Carmen manicurist ended up in the water! Some lucky lady got the box of chocolates I wanted so much! If I'm where I want to be? Not yet, but I'll make it! And my goals now are: work with the doctor and stop smoking! When I thought about taking a break to smoke...

Hi Rose, I'm back... she said, entering again and with a silly smile on her face... it was a friend inviting me to dinner! So, did you think about the questions I asked you? I think I'll have some more tea... (she was elated, as if she had won the lottery!) Friend? I thought... hmmm, there's sausage under that mash! But I kept to myself. I hope it's a nice date for her... so pretty, so sweet! She deserves to be happy!

Yes, I thought about them, doctor... but only in thought, as you said!

Great, Rose... look, it doesn't matter what your answers are. What matters is that, in everything you've thought about, there are probably things you want to change, improve, redo... I don't know! In short, within your answers, there is certainly a tremendous need to send procrastination and self-sabotage to waste. Right?

Know yourself!

You asked me... how can we know if we are self-sabotaging? He was the one who first gave us the best answer to this question... the great Socrates, who you thought worked with polishing... (she laughed!) remember?

Of course, I remember, doctor... I also responded, laughing, a little embarrassed, because that day I had issued a certificate of ignorance with a stamp and signature...

So... the great philosopher said this phrase: "Know yourself", that is, Rose, to know yourself is to reach self-knowledge and, from there, to know all your virtues and all your weaknesses. This self-knowledge will allow you to realize when you are self-sabotaging.

I understand, doctor... does this mean that, by knowing myself, I will know that a bad habit, in fact, is what my brain's autopilot is doing for me?

Exactly that, Rose... she said satisfied... I see you understand. That's why many things, including bad habits, you often do unconsciously. It's a big challenge to change that! And then, of course, comes the burning question: how to deal with this?

The doctor took the words out of my mouth... (the 42 gaze always firm!)

We deal with this, Rose, using emotional intelligence... she said, taking apart my look. Of course, I had no idea what that was! Now, I think I'm smart, sometimes I'm very emotional... so... what?

Rose... I understand that look of doubt in your eyes! Yes, because most of the time we are not trained to have emotional intelligence, which is nothing more than knowing, rationally, how to deal with our emotions. For example: when we have a problem that, at first, we cannot solve, what do we do? You don't even need to answer... generally we blame God and everyone else. Less on ourselves! Because it is much easier to blame others than ourselves. Is not true?

It's true, doctor... whenever I don't get a sale, I blame it on the customer who didn't want to buy. I never ask myself: "Did I approach the client correctly? Why couldn't I convince her to buy the nail polish? Did I do the right thing?" I mean... I never see the problem in myself! I always think that she didn't make the purchase because she's stingy! At the time, I want to say: "Open that bag, lady! Just buy this nail polish... it costs nothing! I mean, it costs money, but it's a bargain...

The doctor laughed... at that point Rose, she said, emotional intelligence would fit like a glove! You don't have to change the client, but rather make changes to yourself! Emotionally, you would have to approach it in a more intelligent way, have a more convincing, more pleasant conversation... in short, convince her that nail polish would be good for her. There is no point in wanting to change the world, because your problems are not its fault. Make changes within yourself and everything around you will change. When we change, we impact our environment, which also changes according to our changes. But to do this you need to know yourself and, from then on, have self-control over all your actions. So, Rose, before wanting to change the world around you, first make changes to yourself.

True, doctor... I said, preparing another one of mine... I'll start without fail on Monday! (She made a sinister face!) I'm joking, doctor, I'm joking...I lose the therapist, but I don't miss the joke. Please continue...

That's right, Rose... she said condescendingly... I must admit that your humor is priceless and that's very good, you know? The ancients already said that laughter is the best medicine. But come on... without self-knowledge, Rose, you end up relying on other people's experiences that end up being influences that don't always serve you, nor will they help you become a better person. Without self-knowledge, you won't be able to know what's best for you, for your life and you'll become a manipulable person... which is quite dangerous.

Dangerous?... I asked, always afraid of those more tense words.

Yes, dear, dangerous...because living without being aware of yourself makes you just work, pay bills, work, pay bills... and what's worse: these external influences make you want things that you may not even need . You just want it because everyone else wants it... and you go after it! Rose...only with self-knowledge will you achieve freedom and leave you in control of your own life.

I understand, doctor...I asked, pouring myself more tea...(if I had some cookies, it would be great!)...and what is the recipe for achieving self-knowledge? I ask this because in theory everything seems easier, right? But I want to see this in practice. Do you have a recipe, a way to achieve self-knowledge?

Of course there is, Rose...she said smiling...but I hope you learned the theory first...

Yes, I understand, Doctor Norma...but learning about self-knowledge only in theory is like making love by correspondence...

Oh! Oh! Oh! Oh Rose...sometimes you surprise me! But you're right! Too much knowledge without practice is just that...theory! But I believe that theory and practice are two sides of the same coin...the difference is that theory is a seed that you plant, and practice is the fruit that you harvest.

Wow, the doctor said it beautifully now! (Would it be time to ask for some cookies? No, no...keep it to yourself!)

How to develop self-knowledge?

Ok, Rose...let's talk about that, that is, let's talk about how you can acquire self-knowledge. After all, you have to earn by what you do...not by what you know. See...the main way to develop self-knowledge is psychotherapy! Of course, this is not free, and the psychotherapy sessions are paid. But see, Rose...investing in this is investing in yourself and your own mental health.

Of course, doctor...I agreed, already fearing that she would charge me for today's conversation. After all, I didn't come to consult. I came to sell a product: me! I think she noticed something in me and started saying:

But that's not your case here now, Rose... our conversation today will be on the house. After all, more than just being a patient, you have already become a great friend. Especially because I was the one who invited you to come here because you had an offer to make me, and I had the afternoon free. But we'll talk about that later...

Phew, doctor...that's good! Because if I had to pay for today's teachings I would be screwed. You know that story about "killing a dog by screaming?" Well then...lately I don't even need to scream...just look at the animal and it falls over! As long as I don't have a steady job...

Ok, Rose...(laughing a lot)...I understand...we'll talk about that later. What I was telling you is that psychotherapy is not a big deal. Today, therapists are even offering online services, which solves the problem of more complicated travel for patients who live far away, etc. Of course, in cases of diagnoses of more serious psychopathologies, face-to-face care is essential.

I understand...I said...(still thinking about the cookies and a cigarette)...and what else can we do, besides psychotherapy, to acquire self-knowledge? Sometimes, I don't know, there's a lack of money or the office is too far away...is there any way for people to do it at home, like exercising? For example...not having money to pay for a gym or an instructor? So, you exercise at home. On YouTube there are a lot of videos teaching how to exercise...

There are several alternatives to complement psychotherapy, Rose...she said, getting up to get a glass jar...would you like some cookies? Have more tea...see, it's shortbread cookies that I love! Take it as you please! (Phew, about time!)

There are some procedures that contribute a lot to the development of self-knowledge... (still standing, she took a table from her desk) that can be done together with psychotherapy. Look...

• **Meditation** – by silencing your mind, you can more easily identify your emotions and, with meditation, you can have control over them.

• **Yoga** – is an ancient practice that will help you unite your body, mind, and spirit and, in doing so, take care of your mental and physical health.

• **Mindfulness** – the best translation for this word is "full attention". These are daily exercises that help you stop doing things on autopilot and pay more attention to them, making more conscious choices. With this technique, you, through meditation, learn to experience the present moment more.

In addition to all this, Rose...it is also advisable to read good books on this subject. If you can, take courses and studies on self-knowledge. Holistic therapy is also a good alternative, which includes psychoanalysis, astral chart, numerology, family constellation, among others.

At that point, after the tea and biscuits, the desire to smoke was unbearable! I was also a little tired with this volume of information about procrastination, self-knowledge...so much so that Dr. Norma noticed my tired look:

Rose...to finish, let me tell you about another important saboteur that works against the development of self-knowledge: idleness! Could you tell me what idleness is?

I think so, doctor...I replied a little insecurely, biting into a cookie...is it like...lazy people?

More or less, dear...look, first I want to make it clear that idleness is not synonymous with laziness. There are differences in the meaning of the two words. Laziness is a defect, right? It puts you down and makes you less than you could be. That's laziness!

It's not my case! I thought, but I didn't say anything. I'm just too lazy to get up in the morning. But...who isn't?

But idleness, Rose...is when you spend your time uselessly or doing nothing. It's when you waste what has always been a true treasure for everyone: time!

Idleness x Productivity

Being idle actually means not producing... being inactive. Of course, this doesn't mean screwing around! Sometimes being idle, after some strenuous work, can be a moment of relaxation, a time to recharge your energy and stimulate your mind. The problem is when idleness goes on for too long... then, yes, it can be harmful and be a symptom of demotivation or even tiredness. Do you spend a lot of time idle, Rose?

Wow...I said laughing...idle, me? Only at night when I watch my soap operas. I won't miss the 9 o'clock for anything in the world, I stop everything I'm doing to watch it. But during the day I'm up and down trying to sell my cosmetics...

That's right, Rose... she replied, smiling... I confess that I too, from time to time, watch a soap opera. But, if you've worked all day, you deserve this moment of leisure, don't you?

True...I agreed...but I could never stay without doing anything for long. I'm very energetic, active...you know what, doctor? Idleness is also tiring... (laughs).

I agree... the important thing, Rose, is to be aware of what you want for your own life. (I want to work here!) Having clear goals and objectives helps you to motivate yourself... only then will your work, whatever it may be, be meaningful to you! Having defined this, it is also important to understand that you will not always be motivated. This is normal! At this point, you have to develop the discipline to achieve your goals.

But doctor...I interrupted...rest and leisure also help the brain, right?

Of course, Rose...rest is essential for better brain development and, of course, to increase your productivity. It is precisely in this aspect that idleness must be used...productively, of course, consciously, that is, it is a time to do nothing...just slow down. (At this moment I turn on the soap opera!)

But in these moments of idleness, Rose, you need to pay attention to two factors: first, avoid self-sabotage due to long unplanned periods of idleness. Second, exaggerated self-demand, wanting to do too much, producing too much...without rest! This is not good! Remember, Rose...everything in life must be treated with balance and harmony.

My grandmother, doctor, always said that anything in excess is bad...I added, taking another cookie...including cookies! (Wow, I almost finished the jar!)

Your grandmother was right...by the way, speaking of working and producing, when can you start?

Start what, Doctor Norma? I asked, already imagining that she was going to complete the sentence: "start stopping eating all the cookies!"

What do you mean, start what?...working here in my office! Isn't that what you were going to propose to me?

Seriously, Doctor Norma??? I asked, almost choking on the doctor's cookies...wow, I can start now if you want!

To keep your "habit" going, I think you can start on Monday! Is that good for you? As for the salary, I'll think of a number that's good for both of us, ok? Although, as for salary, I already know how to resolve that...

What do you mean, doctor?...I asked curiously.

I'll pay you some in cookies, which I've seen are a big hit with you!

I got the message, doctor...I said, taking one more.

We both laughed and talked about the 9 o'clock soap opera!

CHAPTER 6

"The doctor will find a way!"
Caring for the machine

I've been working at Dr. Norma's office for some time now. Guys... after my divorce, I think it was the best thing that happened in my life! I have my own desk, with a flower vase and everything! I have a computer all to myself, with internet and, get this, a jar of butter cookies that smile at me all day long. I, of course, reciprocate. Isn't it incredible? Sometimes, it doesn't even feel like I have a boss... wow, it's even sacrilegious to call the doctor "boss".

In fact, she really is a friend! When there are no clients, she calls me into her office to talk, have coffee... then I tell a few jokes, we laugh a lot, we exchange confidences... it's the kind of job where, every morning, I get up early and go work with joy in my heart. Working is a way of saying it. I don't actually have a job... I have fun! And I get paid for it!

I think it was the Chinese who said that when you do what you love, you will never be working! I mean... this was back in the day when they only made proverbs and... Chinese babies! Nowadays... mercy! There's nothing they won't do! It's all "made in China"!

But look... I know people who would donate a kidney to have a job like mine! That's why I try to do my best here. I'll tell you one thing: if the best part of your job is leaving, then you're in the wrong job. I don't have time to get out! I stay advising the doctor until it's time for her to send me home. "Rose... you're going to miss the soap opera!" Then, yes, I rush out!

Well, as I was saying, I love working with the doctor and I try to do my best. Mainly when I talk to patients waiting for their turn. If they are there it is because they are facing a problem that only therapy can solve. It's as if the doctor's office was the last gas station in the desert and I, of course, end up playing the role of gas station attendant. At first, I thought it was a little strange to hear about patients' problems. I would kind of cut it off by saying, "Don't worry! The doctor will fix it!"

But after a while, after talking to the doctor so much about my own problems, I felt a certain interest in helping people awaken in me too. Of course, not with the doctor's competence but through my own experiences. Add to this the enormous feminine curiosity that is latent in me! If a client starts talking to me before the consultation and starts telling me details about their problem, that's it! The termite of curiosity is starting to eat away at me! I keep wanting to know more and more about the problem...

This was the case of a nurse who confessed to me that she was desperate, even thinking about suicide, because her husband no longer sought her out for sex. Furthermore, she had discovered that the cross-eyed girl from the pharmacy was hitting on her husband. I didn't ask why her husband didn't look for her because it was obvious. In fact, on her face, her breasts, her arms, her legs... she even had a pretty face, but she was fat, very fat! She confessed to me that she had been looking for refuge in food for some time now! I thought it would be better, surreptitiously, to keep the jar of cookies in the cupboard! Geez?

But Nair... I asked... how did you find that out? Does she work at a pharmacy near where you live? Nooooo, girl... she replied distressed... it's in the pharmacy at the hospital where we work. My husband also works at the same hospital as me... he is an X-ray machine operator. But we work different hours. My colleagues on the ward always whisper to me that Zelda is always in and out of his room and sometimes takes a while to leave. He's not a bad husband. He treats me well, there's nothing missing at home... but he's obsessed with this Zelda! And I end up turning a blind eye, because I don't like fighting, arguing... and he knows that!

Who is Zelda? I asked unnecessarily. Who? Well... she replied, rolling her eyes... it's her, the cross-eyed girl who keeps hitting on Olavo. She's not ugly... she said with an air of frustration and envy... she has a pretty body and so on. There's just this problem with her eyes that makes her keep one eye on the priest and the other on the mass. But in the dark, my friend, every cat is brown and Olavo's little room lives in the dark so he can reveal the patients' images. Revealing images and other little things... I'm not stupid, you know? But he'll still regret it, oh yeah, he will!... she mumbled, voice cracking and tears in her eyes.

I thought it was time to cut the conversation short, using my special phrase for these moments: "Don't worry! The doctor will fix it!" While it wasn't her turn, I tried to give some advice, in my own way of course, remembering everything that Dr. Norma had already told me about valuing ourselves, loving ourselves, believing in ourselves. "Don't worry, Nair" ... I said, trying to cheer her up... you'll turn things around. I am sure! Olavo will start to look at you with different eyes, after you start a diet, become hot...

There! Why did I say that? I really am a dumbass! The poor thing burst into tears. She only calmed down when I offered her a cup of coffee and some butter cookies, which she took three at once. Nair, dear... I asked, keeping an eye on the jar... are you calmer? Look, men are really dumb, you know? Olavo doesn't know what a wonderful woman he has at home. Believe me!

Thank you... she replied, sniffling and chewing the cookie... you're the kind one! But I know I'm not attractive to Olavo anymore! Nair... I spoke with some harshness... stop it! That cross-eyed girl is just sex! You are much more than that!

Do you think I should forgive Olavo? she asked, taking another cookie (I started to get worried, another 10 minutes of chatting and she finishes the jar!) Forgive Olavo?... I asked, putting the jar away... No, Nair! We can forgive mistakes! Cheating is not a mistake... it's a choice.

Maybe the doctor would give other advice, but I know what that is! Because my ex, every now and then, would jump over fences too. It's horrible!

At that moment, the office door opened and the patient who was being treated came out. It was Miss

Lenita, a very well dressed, elegant lady, who came out smiling and showing herself very grateful to the doctor for the great consultation! You can come in, dear... said the doctor, addressing Nair and, looking at me, made a sign that this would be the last appointment of the day. I said OKAY and led Mrs. Lenita to the door, while Nair went into the office. It was the 4th time that Miss Lenita came for consultation. She had a serious insomnia problem. Well, now she was very happy and satisfied. Not without reason, I thought, Doctor Norma really is a piece of work.

Wow, Miss Lenita... I said, opening the front door... I'm happy to see you looking so good! Ah, my dear... she replied, going down the steps with the attention and care that age requires... I haven't felt this good in a long time! What doesn't make a good night's sleep, right? (adjusted the silk scarf around her neck) Dr. Norma is a wonderful therapist! The person who recommended it to me was an old friend... Olegário. A few years ago, he came to see her because of noises he said he was hearing... I thought it was because of his huge ears, they must have echoed, I don't know!

Well, I even thought he was going nuts... (he gave a little laugh that sounded more like gargling) ... can you believe, girl, that sometimes he interrupted our conversation asking: "Did you hear that, Lenita?" I kept looking around... "hear what, Olegário?" He would put both hands on his temples and say, "That buzzing... sounds like a doorbell!" And I would go to the door to see if anyone was there... or answer the phone! It was very funny... (adjusted the brooch) ... don't you think?

And was he ok? I asked, walking arm in arm to her car. Oh yeah! she replied, taking the keys out of her huge bag... today Olegário doesn't hear any noise anymore! Because the dead don't hear, they stay there quietly in their graves! I couldn't resist a spontaneous and hearty laugh. She got into the car, rolled down the window and said: I'm joking, my dear... your laugh is proof that my story was worth it! A day without laughing is a wasted day!

It's true... I agreed... but Olegário... really died? Oh, yes... she replied... may God rest his soul. But he died happy and cured of the noise. So much so that before kicking the bucket he would answer the phone even when it wasn't ringing!

We both had a good laugh, and she released the brake and left. I watched the car drive away, thinking "wow, this is how I want to grow old!" Miss Lenita is from the same planet as me! I went back to the office...

Much later, after Nair had left, I went into the doctor's office to plan the next day, as we always did. I went to the pantry to get her a cup of coffee and took the opportunity to bring her the jar of butter cookies. Wow Rose... she said, adding sweetener to the coffee... it seems like you read my thoughts. I really needed a cup of coffee and a cookie. This girl... Nair... left me feeling sad...

Well, Dr. Norma... I said, sitting down... I'm glad you finished with Miss Lenita and called her for the appointment. Otherwise, you would now just be drinking a cup of coffee.

She laughed, bit the tip of the cookie and took a sip of the coffee. This girl has a serious problem... she said, placing the cup on the saucer... we have a lot of work ahead of us! She picked up the cup again and, before taking another sip, said: Nair will need dietary re-education, exercise to lose weight and increase her self-esteem.

That's what I don't understand, doctor... I asked... Nair and I talked a little before the appointment and she, unfortunately, confided in me that she takes refuge in food because of her husband's betrayal. How can we feel less frustrated eating? Look, doctor... if I were to eat every time I felt frustrated or stressed at this point, I would have earned the nickname food inhaler!

Oh! Oh! Oh! Oh Rose... she said laughing... you always have something up your sleeve! Want to know what I think? The thin ones may look good on the scale, but the bigger ones fill out the dress more competently! I said this to Nair... but she, poor thing, will need much more than simple catchphrases! Well, you asked me what food has to do with frustration, right?

I nodded, because I had a whole cookie in my mouth.

You see, Rose... Nair is facing a problem that we call BED, which stands for Binge Eating Disorder, caused by sadness, anxiety, anguish, stress... these are the main triggers that lead a person to acquire this disorder.

BED, I thought, is a good name for a rock band. But I only thought it...

So, food, she continued, works as a kind of escape valve or even as a source of immediate pleasure, when the person feels very distressed or very sad or frustrated.

Wow, doctor... it's Nair's case!

This happens... she said... because food can release hormones and neurotransmitters, such as dopamine, giving the person a feeling of immediate pleasure and relief. But this is a belief, because what is noticed in the long run is the increase in suffering that generated this disorder. The quality of life, of course, will be affected by feelings of failure and sadness.

Nair, Rose, having to face this tremendous emotional adversity, found in overeating a kind of defense mechanism and search for relief from difficulties.

Poor Nair, doctor... I said, taking another cookie... she's going to have to face a lot of struggles from now on, right?

Rose... in fact, we all have this struggle! Our body requires care that requires constant attention and care. In order for us to be successful in life, both personally and professionally, we need to always be attentive, so that we have a *mens sana in corpore sano*!

Oh, doctor... that's Greek to me! I said, taking another cookie. She laughed, taking the last sip of her coffee. No, dear Rose... this is Latin, from the Roman poet Juvenal, who said in the first verse of one of his poems: *"orandum est ut sit mens sana in corpore sano"*.

Oh Lord, Doctor Norma... I asked, making a face... what does that mean? (The only Juvenal I knew was the tire guy near my house!)

This is beautiful Rose! This verse means: *One must ask in prayer for the mind to be healthy in a healthy body*! This poem is actually a kind of prayer about what people should want in life. But Juvenal in his poem makes it clear that, before expressing desires, people must have a healthy mind in a healthy body. By the way, Rose... she said, getting up and taking a book from the shelf... I have this poem here. Can I read a little excerpt to you?

Is it in Latin? I asked, making a strange face... Don't worry, Rose... she said, sitting down... it's translated. Listen to how beautiful this excerpt is. She cleared her throat and said:

One must ask in prayer for a healthy mind in a healthy body.
Ask for a brave soul who lacks the fear of death,
that puts longevity last among blessings
of nature, which supports any type of work,
who knows no wrath, covets nothing and believes more
in the wild labors of Hercules than
in the satisfactions, in the banquets and feather beds of an
oriental king.
I will reveal what you can give yourself:
Certainly, the only path to a peaceful life passes through
virtue.

Rose... she said, closing the book... in a way, this poem draws our attention to what I was talking about, regarding being aware of our daily struggles in defense of our physical and mental health. You know what, Rose? Everyone is very good at taking care of other people's lives... but is everyone also focused on their own life?

I fit my chin between my index finger and thumb and gave that 42 look of mine, which presupposes doubt and the desire to get another cookie.

Food

Rose... we are great at taking care of other people's lives, we give advice to lots of people who might be interested... but do we stop to do the same for ourselves? Taking care of everything here that needs to be taken care of? In fact, good nutrition is one of the secrets to good physical and mental health. But look, Rose... good nutrition is more about quality than quantity! You saw Nair... there is a good example of the binomial quantity versus quality.

Wow... she said that just when I was going to get another cookie.
I gave up right away! My hand, which was on its way to the cookies, hovered
over the jar. To disguise it, I quickly raised my index finger and asked: Ah,
doctor... one question: is it true that too much sugar is bad? (That's the only thing I could think of!).

It's true, she replied... not just sugar, but also salt, especially if they are refined. Actually, Rose, any ultra-processed food, excess fat... these are the big villains that prevent us from having good health. Of course, sometimes we have to eat somewhere other than home... so we are exposed to these foods. In this case, just don't overdo it! After all, a little sugar or a little salt in your diet won't hurt you. Like I said, just don't overdo it.

My grandmother, doctor... I said, interrupting... said that everything in excess is bad, even water! Except money... in fact, the more money the better! I completed taking another cookie, taking advantage of her laughing looking at the ceiling.

Your grandmother was absolutely right, dear...she said... everything in this life depends on balance and having a balanced diet. For example: always prefer natural foods and eat quality vegetables and proteins. They make a huge difference and are the best way to have good health.

You know, doctor... I read on the internet, on a food website, that the best foods that we should eat every day are eggs and bananas. I was happy to read this because eggs and bananas are the two things I eat every day. In fact, doctor, I love to eat... I even think I would join the Taliban if the food was good!

Oh! Oh! Ah!... she laughed heartily... wow Rose, so dramatic! Your good humor always catches me off guard! But see, you mentioned the internet, right? Be aware that you need to be careful with everything you read on the internet. As the internet is a veritable source of free information, we cannot give credit to everything we read. Therefore, always research two or three different sources to confirm whether what you are reading is true or not.

The person who lived on the internet was Otávio, my ex... for him, the answer to everything was on Google. He no longer went to doctors, mechanics... nothing! It was all on Google! After we broke up, I found out, through friends of ours, that he was going on dating sites, the scoundrel! What woman would want that piece of junk? Not even if his semen could cure cancer!

Gross, Rose... ah! oh! ah!... after that one I need another coffee! Is there still some?

I got up and went to the pantry to get some coffee for the doctor. I left her laughing alone. On the way back, I asked if she usually surfed the internet.

Of course, Rose... there is a lot of useful information regarding health information. Just filter it, searching various sources. In fact, we can improve a lot of things in our well-being. But look, Rose... the internet will never replace a healthcare professional or a specialist. The internet is just a support, with information etc. The ideal is to pay for a consultation with a nutritionist so that, by assessing your weight, your body type and health history, he or she can provide you with the nutritional care you need. I referred Nair to a BED specialist.

Physical exercise

But Nair, doctor, in addition to doing this dietary re-education, will have to do a lot of exercise, won't she? I've been told that if you follow a diet without doing physical exercise, your flesh becomes flabby, with your skin falling out everywhere. I have a terrible fear of becoming too fat. Because I'm good with a fork, doctor... that piece of shit of an ex said I didn't have solitary confinement. He said I had an anaconda in my stomach. And that I was only causing losses... etc.

Rose... moaned the doctor, cackling... stop, because otherwise I'm going to pee right here!

It's true, doctor... I continued... but I like to eat! I eat for pure pleasure! Hence my fear of gaining weight like Nair! The other day I went to a gym that is on the way here from the office. Wow, doctor, I dragged myself out of there... with pain all over my body... and I just went to ask for the price!

She stood up abruptly and ran to the bathroom. Rose... she shouted from inside... you'll kill me this way! Oh! Oh! Oh!

When she came back, she was composed. She sat wiping away a tear with a piece of paper towel. Oh, Rose... always something with you! But you're right! Practicing physical exercise and proper nutrition are the best way to a healthy life. By acting like this, we increase that feeling of well-being, improve the cardiorespiratory system, strengthen muscles and many other benefits, such as, for example, improving self-esteem!

The important thing is to go slowly, especially if you are not used to exercising or perhaps do not have this habit. I, for example, never skip my walks. Three times a week, a 45-minute walk. It's ideal... and you can do it in two installments: in the morning 20 minutes and in the afternoon 25 minutes or vice versa!

Oh, doctor, the most I've done in this regard is getting up in the morning. My best time from bed to bathroom is 1m20s... but it can be improved!

Oh! Oh! Oh! You are too much... but, look Rose, do what I suggested and gradually increase it, as you enjoy it. Then you can progress to light, short distance running. Increase as your breathing capacity also increases. Rose... running is good for losing weight, toning your thighs, staying in shape, and working on muscular endurance. But you see... walking or running is not just about keeping your body in shape. Walking or running is best for the brain in terms of mood, memory and learning.

And going to a gym, doctor... is it worth it? At that gym I told you about, I felt very frustrated. There were only hot girls on those machines and a bunch of guys with a lot of tattoos, a lot of muscle and, I believe, little brains! Everyone with a beautiful, toned body... could I achieve that too?

Of course you can, dear... in this case we are talking about weight training, which is important to do correctly.

That's why a gym is important! There are professionals who will guide you to have the correct posture when performing each exercise. This professional will establish the best routine for you, according to your goals.

Depression? No! Bad eating habits!

As you see, Rose, I told you about the two great pillars that support good health for our body: good and adequate nutrition and physical exercise. Mainly food, which, directly or indirectly, is linked to our emotions. It's true! See... there are people who believe they will never get sick. This belief is so false that these people, at the slightest sign of a negative emotion, already think they are sick.

Much of what we feel on a daily basis is closely linked to our diet. For example, too much caffeine and foods high in sugar can make a person anxious. The coffee that I buy here for the office is decaffeinated! A diet based on eggs, grains, fruits, nuts, vegetables, fish... makes the body produce serotonin and dopamine, which are the well-being hormones. Also, foods rich in vitamin B fight depression.

Doctor... I interrupted... you talked about what we can eat. So, what should I cut out of my diet to avoid these risks of anxiety and depression? Is it a lot to cut?

Rose... you have to cut out all foods made with vegetable oils, for example, because they are polyunsaturated. I'm talking about soybean, corn, sunflower, canola oils...

I only use canola oil, doctor... I interrupted again... it's more expensive but I think it's the best! I said, thinking I was saying something important!

My God, Rose... she said impressed... stop using that. Canola doesn't even exist in nature. It's an acronym, dear, that stands for Canadian Oil Low Acid. A real poison for your health, like any other vegetable oil. These oils release free radicals that harm our cells. We have to do what our grandparents did: cook with pork lard, which is healthier and more economical.

Also cut out foods' rich in sugar or sodium, such as fast foods, canned and packaged foods, such as cookies like Oreos... all of this causes vitamin and mineral deficiencies and causes that feeling of fatigue and irritability.

Everything I like, doctor... and love eating! If you have anything else I need to cut let me know... because now, just cutting your wrists too!

Geez, Rose... ah! oh! oh! Do not exaggerate! A cookie or a cheeseburger every now and then won't kill anyone. Just don't make it a habit! Another thing, Rose... never stop drinking water, the most critical and important element for human life. It regulates our temperature and is essential for all of our body's functions. Rose... did you know that 60 to 70% of our weight is made up of water?

I didn't know, doctor... but my ex's body was definitely made up of 60 to 70% vodka and whiskey. In fact, when he dies, no one will know whether to bury, cremate or bottle him! (the doctor had to go to the bathroom again!)

Oh, Rose... she said, coming back and still laughing... I just discovered how important you are for my diuretic functions. But continuing... like I said, our body is 70% water, right? So, we have to keep this water clean by drinking at least two liters of water every day. An elderly person, for example, who does not drink enough water may start to forget things, names, paths... this is sometimes confused with Alzheimer's but, most of the time, it is dehydration!

I started laughing and the doctor, of course, asked why. I told her about an old man who had gone to the doctor because, lately, he was forgetting everything. And he said to the doctor: "Doctor... I don't know, you tell me something and I instantly forget it!" The doctor then asked him: "And since when have you been like this?" The old man looked at the doctor with a blank face and asked: "Like what, doctor?"

There the doctor went, again, running to the bathroom!

CHAPTER 7

Who do you think you are?

(Where is your attention now?)

Today I woke up on cloud 9! As soon as I woke up, after tapping the clock radio bell, I said to myself: "Rosemary... today is going to be another great day!" It even rhymed! But, in fact, after I started working at Dr. Norma's office, I've been waking up happy. Happy because it's my best job and the doctor is the best boss of all I've ever had!

She is great with me and treats me as if I were her "protégé". In fact, there are times when I don't know if I'm an employee or a patient. In fact, she is the patient, because dealing with me requires patience! At the end of the day, when we talk over coffee, she doesn't miss the opportunity to encourage me with wonderful advice.

Lately, she has been really encouraging me to go back to school! Damn... at these times I get stuck. Going back to school? Only God and I know how I managed to finish high school... it was more or less like drunkenly climbing a hill, in tripping and stumbling! The first time she talked about it, she quoted that Greek philosopher, Socrates, who said: if someone wants to be complete, they have to study, work and fight. Well, working and fighting is what I've been doing every day, but studying...

When I think about going back to studying, I start to feel all the difficulties that I will certainly face. And then that laziness hits... but I'm not lazy! I like working, doing, undoing... I like staying active. But I don't feel that enthusiasm when it comes to studying. I think my laziness is mental! Actually, I feel like I'm lazier in my spirit than in my body.

But listening to the doctor, I learned that, instead of seeing difficulty in every opportunity, we should see a challenge in every difficulty.

This is a beautiful phrase! Interesting and stimulating! But I think I need more than a good sentence to make me go back to studying. I only think about the challenges that lie ahead, since it has been more than a year since I stopped studying. That's all I think about! But I just think... and when the doctor starts to insist on this, I go into airplane mode! I don't say anything, I just keep thinking... thinking...

The other day, over coffee in the late afternoon, she told me about my thoughts. She said that everything we think, directly or indirectly, influences our actions and feelings. Therefore, it was not good to think about studying as a difficulty...

Rose... she asked... do you know how many thoughts you have per day? Wow, doctor... I replied... I think it would be the same as counting how many times I blink per day. Impossible to know! I think the thought process is the same with thoughts!

Ah! ah! Ah!... laughed the doctor... you're not wrong, dear! In fact, it seems almost impossible for us to count our thoughts. But you should know that, according to a study carried out by a university in California, a person has around 12 to 60 thousand thoughts per day.

Now look... according to these experts, who carried out this study, at least 80 to 90% of these thoughts are useless, she added. I imagine so... I said... 12 to 60 thousand thoughts a day? I get tired just thinking about it...

Look Rose... this tiredness is a reality! You've heard the expression "mental fatigue", right? Well... the act of thinking requires effort in the same way that physical effort requires.

That's what I don't understand, doctor... I started asking... sometimes I think about a problem so much that, in the end, I feel so tired... as if I were Cinderella after completely cleaning the castle and... without help from the birds! Why is that?

The brain, Rose... she replied, laughing... is naturally lazy because thinking uses a lot of energy. When you force yourself to think too much about the same task, you end up causing what we call mental fatigue. Then comes that feeling of exhaustion, difficulty concentrating, motivation... in this state we are unable to progress and even our ability to make decisions is compromised. Sometimes, Rose, mental fatigue is an even stronger sensation than physical tiredness! Believe it!

I believe it! But doctor... I asked... how can this be explained? A thought is so... I don't know... invisible, untouchable... it has no weight, no color, you can't keep it in your bag for later use... do you understand me? How can this make us tired?

Rose... she said, pouring herself another cup of coffee... first let's try to understand what a thought is.

Yes... I said, holding my chin with my index finger and thumb (I love this pose!) giving that 42 look... and what is a thought, doctor?

Rose... she said, returning the cup to the saucer... if you open the dictionary and look for the word *thought* you will find a simple answer, like: "the act of thinking or considering something, an idea or opinion or, even, a set of ideas on a given subject." However, Rose, when it comes to conceptualizing what a thought is, this is very little, very shallow.

I understand, doctor, it would be like looking at the tip of the iceberg without seeing the huge block of ice underneath, right?... I asked, proud of the precision of my example.

Exactly, dear... she replied smiling... the dictionary entry is just the tip of your iceberg. Listen... do we still have shortbread cookies? Yes, we do... I replied, getting up to pick up the pot... today wasn't Nair's day to come here for a session with you.

From the kitchen I heard her laughing... I also kept thinking that, if the captain of the Titanic had known a little more about icebergs, that whole tragedy would have been avoided and James Cameron and Di Caprio wouldn't have made all that money! I came back from the kitchen with the jar of cookies... here you go, doctor, another cup of coffee?

Yes, I do, Rose... please... oh! Thank you... see dear, as I said, conceptualizing thought is something very complex. But I could start by explaining to you that, as the human species evolved, the brain also evolved along with it, even increasing in size. In this process, the number of neurons also increased, causing brain functions to become increasingly... let's say, more robust, more effective! Thinking is nothing more than one of those functions that emerged and was improved as the brain evolved more and more.

Okay, doctor... I agreed... but I still don't understand how thoughts are formed. How is it born? For example... it's just a comparison, okay? When we accidentally stick a splinter in our hand or step on something sharp, we feel a sharp pain, right? At these times I use the most vicious swear words and my body, I think, begins a process of... I don't know... defense. Then, in the place of the wound, a small wound begins to form, sometimes with pus... which is nothing more than my body finding a way to resolve itself.

I don't understand what you're getting at, Rose! she said, taking a cookie.

I'll try to explain myself, doctor! What I meant was that the red around the wound, the swelling and that yellow pus... all of this was my body doing on its own, without me asking. I think thoughts are born in the same way... they come into our heads like the electricity or water bill... without us asking!

Oh! Oh! Oh! Only you... said the doctor, laughing... but look, Rose... thoughts don't come from nothing. There must be an electrochemical reaction between the neurotransmitters and the nerve cells, which are billions of neurons. We call this reaction a synapse, which is the means that neurons use to communicate with neurotransmitters.

Synapse to me sounds like the name of a drink... I thought, but didn't say it... I even see a bartender asking the customer: "Drink, sir?" "Yes, please... give me a shot of synapse with lemon and ice!" "Right away… do you prefer the Russian synapse or the domestic one?" "Hmm...

I prefer the Russian one, with lots of ice!" I started to laugh inside, but the doctor noticed...

What are you laughing at, Rose? she asked with a slight smile. Nothing, doctor... I replied... I was just thinking about this complicated thing that is thought. It makes you want to stop thinking... what a hassle!

I know you, Rose... she said, pouring more coffee... you were thinking about something funny. But tell me later, because, you know, I like to laugh too. But let's continue... I like this theme: thoughts!

Many people think that thoughts are just ideas that come out of our brain or sentences that come out of our mouth. In fact, Rose, thoughts are more than that. I would say that the great powerhouse, from which our thoughts are born, are our senses. Everything we see, hear, feel, touch... generates thoughts. Thus, thoughts are nothing more than scenes that represent our reality. They are related to our critical sense! They even allow us to elaborate perceptions, emotions, feelings and any and all meanings we give to objects, experiences, memories, images and events. Thinking helps us interpret the environment around us.

You talked about memories... I said, taking a cookie... I mean, not only my senses produce thoughts but everything I remember too, right? For example... I just remembered that tomorrow is Nair's day to come for a session. Maybe we should provide more shortbread cookies... don't you think? She always takes it three at a time...

Ah! Ah! Ah!... well thought out, dear! In fact, you touched on an important point: memory plays a fundamental role in thinking, as it allows the retrieval of important information! Thinking also allows us to accumulate information, helping us to make decisions in the present and, of course, even to plan the future.

I understand, doctor... I said... but thinking is easy. It's really difficult to act. I think the biggest difficulty is that we act according to what we think. I think a lot when you tell me to go back to school. I really think... I can see how important it would be for me, for my life... but when I think about taking action... yes, God helps us! I don't think I can handle it!

Rose, pay attention... she said gravely, leaning back in the armchair, crossing her legs and putting her palms together as if she were going to pray... do you know where the root of all our failures is? It lies in the fact that you keep thinking: "Oh, I am useless! Oh, I am weak!" "Oh, this"... "Oh, that"... Stop it, my child... (Wow, my heart sunk on that one! My child?") Rose... it's essential that you start thinking in a firm and powerful way… "Whatever it is, I can do it!" "Whatever it will be, I can do it!"… do it without pretension, without ostentation or worry.

I'll do it mom... I mean, doctor! From now on I will think about my studies in a more practical, more objective way and... on Monday I will go to a course so I can take the entrance exam and...

That's right, Rose... she said enthusiastically... in fact, this type of thinking has a name: it's called...

Practical thinking: this is when you stop with abstraction and theory and move on to practice. This means leaving the sphere of thought and putting your goals into practice. There are other types of thoughts, Rose, see:

Analytical thinking: this is when you gather all the information about your goal, in your case going back to school, and weigh the pros and cons. This analysis helps you find the best option. What college will I go to? Where will I do it? etc.

Systems thinking: this allows you to understand all the small details of your goal. Let's say you intend, like I did, to study Psychoanalysis. With systems thinking you will discover small facts about human behavior and mental processes, brain functioning, memory, etc. You will understand that these details are part of a larger system and understand a larger dimension of reality.

Creative thinking: this thinking concerns innovation. It allows you to create new ways of approaching a problem. You Rose, with your good humor and insight, in my opinion, would make an excellent psychoanalyst.

Certainly, you would create new approaches in treating mental problems.

Logical thinking: this is thinking oriented towards the logical chain of ideas and arguments. These ideas and arguments, in general, are indisputable and help in understanding the world and everyday problems. It is formed by two important forms of rationalization:

- **Deductive thinking**: allows you to take an indisputable fact and apply it to specific cases. For example: All dogs bark. If Rex barks, Rex is a dog.
- **Inductive thinking**: this is the opposite. Allows you to pick up multiple specific cases and transform them into an indisputable fact. For example: all dogs I know, bark. Therefore, every dog barks.

Wow, doctor, I think this deductive thinking thing is awesome. These dog examples are incredible. I remember when I had Philosophy in high school, my teacher, Miss Carmelita, said some things like that.

It's true, Rose... she said... this is a very recurring theme in Philosophy classes. Did you like Philosophy?

Yes, I liked it... until the day when Miss Carmelita asked me for an example of logical deduction. I got up from my desk and said: "Every chair is a piece of furniture!" Very well, Rosy... that's a true premise. Complete your deduction now for the whole class. Let's see! I cleared my throat and added: "I have pain in the chairs, so I have pain in the furniture!" The whole class burst into laughter... except Miss Carmelita, of course, who told me to go and cure my "pain in the chairs" in the principal's office.

Oh! Oh! Oh! Rose... this teacher didn't have the slightest sense of humor! I would have given you a zero in Philosophy, but a huge 10 in creativity! This is very good, really good and...

Doctor... I interrupted... without wanting to cut her off, and already cutting her off, is it possible to control our thoughts? I mean... select the best ones and reject the bad ones? Because in my mind, thoughts come as if it were a busy street and I, on the corner, was looking for a boyfriend... difficult to see who is who, who is the most handsome, the most intelligent, the one with the most attractive smile, the best dressed... how do I stay focused?

Your comparison is good, Rose... she said laughing... an unfocused mind lost in several objectives tends to have a whirlwind of conflicting thoughts. The focused mind knows what it wants and doesn't get lost in abstractions. A good tool for controlling thoughts is...

Meditation

Rose... this is one of the most effective activities for controlling thoughts. It is a practice of regulation and synchronization of the body and mind, which trains the focus of attention to achieve tranquility, concentration, reduction of stress and anxiety. Of course, and it will help you achieve your main goal, which is to attend college.

With you talking about meditation, I remember those Hindus with turbans, sitting cross-legged looking into space...

Yes, Rose... this is meditation, but Hindus take meditation to another level, much deeper... their intention is to reach nirvana, that is, to obtain full knowledge of oneself and reach total enlightenment and...

Nirvana? Better would be to reach the Beatles or Led Zeppelin. I don't really like Nirvana much!

Oh! Oh! Oh! My God, Rose... the Hindus' nirvana is different. It has nothing to do with rock bands! Reaching nirvana, for Hindus, is reaching a complete state of self-actualization, that is, complete happiness and bliss. In our case, we use meditation for physical and mental relaxation, to reduce anxiety, improve breathing, mood and create more energy for everyday activities and, of course, control our thoughts.

Interesting, doctor... I said... I like that idea. I just don't know how to stay in that typical meditation pose. I have the feeling that if I cross my legs like that, I'll never be able to uncross them and get back to normal. Even more so, having both hands on your knees and your fingers making that sign that, for me, means something else. You know?

Oh, Rose... said the doctor, laughing heartily... I'm going to end up peeing right here. Oh! Oh! Oh! But look... another day we'll talk more in depth about meditation, okay?

Okay... I agreed... and you know, doctor, I came to the conclusion that I want to go to college for Psychoanalysis. I want to be like you!

Well, look, Rose... I feel vain to be a reference for you. But, in truth, I wanted to be like you with your priceless good humor. Well, you can count on me in this endeavor of yours. I will help you with whatever is necessary, because, even without objectively realizing it, you help me a lot and I am very grateful to have you here with me.

Wow, doctor... I said, kind of emotional... never, since the time when I was still potty training, have I felt so happy in my life! Thank you for everything!

Thank you for what? Rose, dear... last advice: always say what you think with hope. Think in what you do with faith. And do what you must do with love. What's left is profit... now let's go, it's time for our soap opera...

I left feeling on cloud nine...

CHAPTER 8

Meditation
(Every day, I get better and better!)

Believe it or not, I started studying again! I signed up for a course and now, under the healthy and maternal support of Dr. Norma, I am preparing to take an entrance exam and thus enter college (In Brazil, they are required to take entrance exams to get into college and receive scholarships). In fact, it's already been decided: I want to major in psychology and then take a good psychoanalysis course. Just like the doctor!

But I confess... it's not easy! I'm feeling like that rocket that, after a long time in space, has to return to Earth. If it reenters at once, it could explode! That's why it has to go around the planet and, slowly, penetrate the atmosphere. It has to sneak in!

Me too... I'm re-entering the academic world on the sly. Because otherwise I'll end up exploding. Reviewing, dealing with, and studying subjects that I haven't seen in a long time is proving complicated. Portuguese, Mathematics, Science, Geography, History... there are so many things to study that it's crazy! Sometimes it gets discouraging! At these times, it's impossible not to remember the doctor's words: "Rose"... she said once... "no one goes crazy from studying so much. It's easier to go crazy from being ignorant"!

You can't disagree with a statement like that, right?! She keeps telling me that studying is the light of life, it's our greatest strength, etc... but I feel like I have to save energy when it comes to "we'll see"! It's been a struggle taking the course. In Portuguese classes, for example, I am nothing more than a hidden subject without any predicate. So far, I've only managed to get one direct object... Percy the Portuguese teacher, a wonderful hunk... a noun full of good adjectives!

In fact, he was the one who made me discover that I had nothing to do with the sciences field. I like Geography, History, Languages... but Mathematics, Physics, Chemistry, Biology... they are to me in the same way that a guitar soloist is to a circle of orchestra players. But there's no other way... if I want to pass an entrance exam, I have to study all of this too. As that idiot of my ex used to say... "if you want to eat my feijoada (Brazilian dish), you have to drink my cachaça (Brazilian liquor)!"

When it's Mathematics class, I feel reduced to an ordinary fraction. Professor Ganymede is an old man who must be as old as the pyramids. A sadist, similar to Mr. Potato Head, who experiences orgasms when he asks me to go to the blackboard and solve an equation. At these times I want to die from Covid and yellow fever from having to enter, in front of everyone, into a melee with a 2nd grade equation. I look at the equation with enormous dislike... and it reciprocates! After a few seconds, this round-faced executioner says: "Go sit down, girl! Does anyone know?" I go sit with everyone looking at me like I'm a leper in a kissing booth!

But I like science classes. The teacher is cute... tiny, cute... so much so that she has already earned the nickname Pituca. Her classes are a delight! My colleague, Alaor, is lost! The other day he told me, sighing, that Pituca, as a science teacher, is the most beautiful specimen of a vertebrate mammal... a fantastic set of head, trunk, and limbs. He said that, if he could, he would embalm Pituca and put her on a keychain... just to be with him. Geez! Go be creepy like that at home!

But that's it... from Monday to Friday, after finishing work at the office, I go to school at night. It's been tough, but I'm glad I have the doctor who has been giving me a lot of strength and courage to continue and not give up. She always tells me that studying is good, and that the important thing is not to study to live but, rather, to live to study.

She also says that studying is not a waste of time. Studying is investing time. At these times she always remembers a phrase from the philosopher Socrates. The last thing she said to me was: "We have to study and face challenges, because a life without challenges is not worth living."

What I absolutely cannot do is lose focus... it's bad enough I'm missing the soap opera! But it's hard to stay focused with so many things going on around me! Especially in times of internet! For example, I open the computer and start researching for, I don't know, some school project. In that moment I'm focused on the subject I have to research.

But then I go through Facebook and take a look at the posts... that's it! My focus has lost its way, because I have an irresistible desire to browse, look at photos, offers, cute puppies, kittens, babies who play the piano, blind people who practice target shooting, magical herbs that lose weight... another click takes me to Instagram and it's the same thing; Another click and I'm already on WhatsApp exchanging ideas with the school group... and so on! The research? Well, the research... I'll do it tomorrow! And it's always like this...

I told Dr. Norma about this, and I was immediately scolded! What do you mean, Rose... she asked... are you that determined, courageous, bold woman that I know... or are you a rat?

I didn't respond... I just felt a huge desire to eat cheese. She, of course, noticed that I was completely embarrassed and had no response. Rose... she said gently and already switching into maternal mode... if you change the focus, you change the direction. If you change your thoughts, you will change your behavior. Change the direction and you will change the results... things, dear, only change for those who change! Do you understand?

I just shook my head, embarrassed and, before I said anything, she added: Rose... the only person who can change your future is yourself. So, believe in yourself and make your dream a reality!

Yes, I know, doctor... I replied with a somewhat choked voice and with my eyes wanting to shed a tear... I just don't know how to do it. It feels like something stronger than me takes me out of focus. Just one small obstacle and I...

Rose... she cut me off, placing her hand on my shoulder... a few days ago I promised you that I would talk more deeply about meditation. I think this is the time... because meditation is the best technique for developing balance, discipline, and focus. Now that you're back to studying, you need exactly that: balance, discipline, and focus! You will make it, I promise! You will be able to make your dream come true and, by studying hard and determinedly, you will be the best psychoanalyst!

Hearing these words, I felt motivated! Great doctor Norma... only she can push me up! Thank you, doctor... I said, moved... if it weren't for you, I don't know what would become of me!

Well, Rose... you make me emotional! Consider me just a teacher... just like the many you've had!

But you are different, doctor... I replied... very different from my teachers! Especially the ones I had when I was a kid. They said: "Rosy... without studying, your life will suck!" As I was a child, I didn't know what to respond. But today... well, today I know that I don't need anything else... just studying makes me crazy!

Oh! Oh! Oh! Oh Rose... she said laughing... you and your jokes! What time is the next appointment? I want to start talking to you about meditation today...

I left her room and went to get my planner. There's only one more today, doctor... I said, showing her the planner... and guess what! Today there's Nair at 4:30pm. I better stock up the cookie jar...

She laughed and said that after Nair we would talk about meditation. It will work, I thought, because the consultation lasts from 45 minutes to an hour. We'll be able to talk a lot until 6pm and I won't be late for the course. I went to my desk at the reception to greet Nair when she arrived.

Did not take too long. When she arrived, I was studying Portuguese and hearing Professor Percy's voice in my head. She walked into the reception and my jaw dropped to the carpet! It was another Nair... she looked beautiful, wearing black fabric pants and a yellow linen blouse, a V-neck highlighting a slight cleavage, bag and low-heeled shoes matching the whole outfit... anyway, she was no longer bigger, disheveled hair, chubby face like when she came, all collapsed, to see the doctor three months ago. When she came here for the first time, Nair had more tires than a tire shop! But now... Jesus, Mary, and Joseph... what a change! She wasn't skinny... but she was thick!

Wo-wow, Nair... I said, standing up and without those cordial exaggerations... you look beautiful! Oh, Rose... she said shyly... you'll make me feel embarrassed!

No, don't sit down yet... I said, holding her arm... take a spin. I want to see better how wonderful you look! She greeted me with a coquettish expression, as if she were on a catwalk. Oh, Rose... she smiled... stop it... look, I'm already blushing!

Stop being silly, Nair... as my ex would say: "You look the way the devil likes and God, on top of that, blesses you!" Speaking of which, what about Olavo, your husband? How has he been dealing with all this change?

Oh, Rose, you won't believe it... she said, smiling as if she had a hanger in her mouth... he's more homely now and looks at me like a cat looking into an aquarium. But do you want to know? I don't care... you know, Rose? As I started to change my look (which only God and I know how much work it took!) and then I started to groom myself better, taking more care of my appearance... Olavo started losing importance to me! I was changing on the outside and... you see... I was changing on the inside! I remembered the doctor's words...

But what about the cross-eyed girl from the pharmacy... I asked in amazement... are they still messing around? I don't know, Rose... she replied with impressive confidence... and I don't even want to know! Thanks to Dr. Norma, I learned to value myself more, to have higher self-esteem. I don't know... I became more selective. You learn to choose what is best for you and Olavo, Rose, I discovered that he is not the best for me. Of course, I haven't stopped being his wife yet... I take care of the house, the food, his clothes... but I no longer feel interested in continuing to be his wife. The truth, Rose, is that I fell out of love with Olavo.

Come on, Nair... I said with a wink... there has to be a motivation for us to stop loving someone. Who is he? Tell me everything and don't hide anything from me!

She sat down, placed her bag on her knees and, smiling and rolling her eyes, exclaimed like a Hindu pronouncing his own mantra: Jethro...

Jethro?... I exclaimed... what an exotic name, Nair! (I didn't say anything, I just thought it... it sounded like a car name to me: "Jethro has arrived... the new Volkswagen sedan! I was laughing inside!) It's a biblical name... she explained to me... he comes from a family of evangelicals. He is very nice, polite and it was thanks to him that I lost weight on my body, but I gained, you see, weight on my conscience. Now I feel sorry for Olavo because, from the way the carriage is going, my marriage will soon go to hell!

No way, girl... but where did you meet Jethro? Jethro... she corrected, frowning... he works at the gym I go to. He is, let's say, a class trainer. He teaches the exercises, how to use the equipment and so on. After going there for a while, he started to pay me special attention and I also started to feel attracted to him.

But tell me, Nair... I asked, curious... has anything more serious happened between you two? Well... she said, kind of blushing... one time he invited me to have a coffee in the cafeteria opposite and... oh, Rose...

I don't believe it, Nair... my eyes widened... did you go to town? Nooooo, girl... she was surprised... it was just a kiss... but I felt like something was mixing between us. Nair, the name of that is saliva... I said, sitting next to her. We exchanged a laugh and I, of course, started asking: What else? What else? Nothing else... she said resolutely... I don't want to do to Olavo what he did to me. I'm not like that! I told him that, something more serious, only after I separated.

Of course, Nair, of course... I agreed... and did he understand? Didn't keep insisting? Nope, Rose... she replied excitedly... he understood right away and even praised me and that he would be waiting for me, can you believe it? Look... she said, opening her bag and taking out her cell phone... I'll show you a photo of him that I took at the gym. What do you think? Wow, Nair... I exclaimed, taking her cell phone... how handsome, huh?

This Jethro guy was a mountain of muscles. Very buff and no tattoos. Well, he was an evangelical and this group thinks that tattoos are a thing of Satan. But the guy had a body that... with just one of his thighs I could run a butcher shop! His breakfast must be cornflakes and iron filings. On the back of his neck should be written: "Does not contain gluten but contains glutes." And those glutes would make a great barbecue for the entire gym! I thought Percy was much prettier. He's not as muscular as Jethro, but he has those green eyes... I think I would go for a walk in the Gaza Strip if he invited me!

Of course, I spared Nair of those comments. I returned the cell phone just saying: He's a handsome man, Nair! But look... don't let your heart lead you. Privilege your brain too and never forget: the most important person for you is yourself! Talk about it with the doctor...

I'll do it, Rose... she said, putting her cell phone in her bag... don't worry! Could you let the doctor know I'm here? Of course... I said, looking at the clock... in fact, she was waiting for you. I got up and knocked twice on the door, opening it. Hi doctor... Nair is here! You can go in, Nair... I said... do you want coffee? A water? She shook her head and went inside.

I closed the door, sat at my desk, and picked up my Portuguese module. But I couldn't study properly... I kept thinking about the miracles that a gym can do, when you have discipline, determination, and focus! I also thought about my Portuguese teacher... it gave me a strange feeling. I don't know...

Nair stayed with Dr. Norma for almost an hour. When she came out, she was smiling and exuding happiness! I took her to the door, and she said goodbye to me, giving me the biggest hug. Thank you, Rose... she said softly... you and the doctor are very important to me. After Jethro, right?... I asked jokingly with her. She responded with a laugh and, slinging her bag over her shoulder, headed down the sidewalk. I watched her walk away, thinking: what doesn't make for good therapy, huh?

I went back inside, and Dr. Norma was leafing through my Portuguese module. I miss my student days... she said... with an expression of sincere nostalgia.

Wow, Rose... she said, closing my book... did you see how wonderful Nair is? Dang... I feel so satisfied when I see the good results of therapy. Don't you? Yes, I do... I replied... but I was more impressed by the fact that she didn't ask for shortbread cookies...

Oh! Oh! Oh! Rose... said the doctor, laughing... how perceptive you are! I offered her cookies during our conversation... and she refused saying that her diet was serious and that she could not waver! Do you know what this is, Rose?

I already know what you're going to tell me: determination, discipline, and focus... I responded with some conviction. That's right, Rose... she replied... Nair showed us everything that can be achieved with determination, discipline, and focus. That's exactly what I'd like to talk to you about today. Let's go into the office and sit down... ah! bring a cup of coffee!

I poured her a cup of coffee and, of course, another for myself. I sat in the armchair and she in the other. She took a sip of coffee and placed the cup on the table. Rose... she began, putting her fingers together... it was a happy coincidence that Nair came today, because she is determined, disciplined, and focused and this has everything to do with the topic I want to explain to you: meditation!

I'm all ears, doctor... I said, trying to get Percy out of my head... when it comes to concentration, I don't think I got off to a good start.

Let's go! Meditation, Rose, is a very old technique, ancient I would say, that helps you develop concentration and focus, in addition to promoting other benefits. But concentration and focus are what you need most at the moment to continue your studies and be successful.

That's true, doctor... I agreed, still not really understanding what meditation is... what are the other benefits of meditation?

Wow, Rose... there are many! For example: it makes you have a calmer mind; improves your memory, develops your attention and focus; increases your productivity; reduces stress and anxiety; with meditation you deal better with negative emotions and physical pain and many others that, as we talk, I will remember. The important thing to know now is that, in meditation, you are the protagonist of your thoughts. It makes you get in touch with your essence and stay away from material things.

Wow, Doctor Norma... I exclaimed... how cool! I like the idea of having control over my thoughts. In fact, I'm already like that, you know?... I lied, still trying to scare off Percy who was swimming in my head. I don't know, Rose... she said seriously... without meditation it's very difficult for us to have control over our thoughts. Do you understand?

I remained silent looking at her, kind of frozen. Do you understand, Rosy? I heard Percy ask me, next to the board, looking at me. Rose?... asked the doctor, laughing and picking up the cup of coffee... are you there?

Oh, doctor, I'm sorry... I said, eyes widening... you're right... it's very difficult to control our thoughts. My mind went somewhere else...

Well then, Rose... concentration is one of the great benefits of meditation. It will help you, firstly, to get to know yourself better. Because meditation is nothing more than taking a powerful magnifying glass and observing very closely the behavior patterns that happen within you.

Magnifier?... I thought but didn't say it, but to me it sounds like the name of a disease. "So-and-so died from a magnifier... it was horrible! It started on the neck and... oh my God, concentrate Rose, concentrate...

A magnifier is a magnifying glass, right, doctor?... I asked, trying to show concentration. Exactly, dear... she replied... but it's just a comparison of how meditation will help you get to know yourself better and develop balance, discipline, and focus. Plus, it helps you sleep better and relax more deeply.

I understand, doctor... I said, drinking coffee... but how do you meditate? How to do it? Do I have to have any special equipment like a mat, for example? Incense? Another question: am I at risk of any health problems? Does...

No, Rose... she cut me off, appeasing my anxiety and grabbing a cookie... you don't need anything to meditate. Just you! There is also no contraindication, regardless of age or lifestyle. What you have to do is disconnect from everything and start a meditation routine. This will require persistence and patience... until practice leads to habit. So far so good, Rose? Any questions?

No, doctor... I also responded, taking a cookie (I'm glad Nair didn't accept any. The jar was full!) As for persistence, I can guarantee it... but as for patience, I don't know! I'm very impatient, doctor!

Rose, dear... persistence and patience are fundamental in meditation. Let's talk a little about each one separately, okay? Let's go...

Persistence

I always compare the act of meditating with the act of going to a gym, that is, it requires training and effort, but it is not impossible. Meditation also requires training and effort... perhaps the first few days, with these new habits in your routine, will be difficult. But time is your friend, Rose!

As Max Weber, the great German intellectual and founder of Sociology, said: *Man would not have achieved the possible if, repeatedly, he had not attempted the impossible.* Confucius, the great Chinese philosopher also said something about persistence. I think it's great! Listen... Carry a handful of dirt every day and you will make a mountain! Isn't it beautiful, Rose?

I liked the German's phrase better, doctor... I said... it seems more "down to earth" to me! As for the Chinese phrase... I don't know... take a handful of dirt each time? Well, hire an excavator... it takes less time! Doesn't it? Oh! Oh! Oh! Oh Rose... she said laughing... this phrase is just symbolic to explain persistence!

Look doctor... I said, happy to see Dr. Norma laugh... what I really like about the Chinese is yakisoba and checkered chicken! That's on payday, of course! That's right, Rose... she said, still laughing... but let's talk about patience! OK? Look:

Patience

Look... even though it may seem contradictory, people who start meditating are not exempt from losing their patience. It's common to want to feel the benefits in the first few seconds, which, of course, doesn't happen. That's why it's important to avoid judgment and enjoy the moment, laugh at yourself, and learn to listen to yourself.

I understand... I took another cookie and teased... isn't there a phrase to talk about patience, doctor? Yes, there is, Rose... she said... have you ever heard of the Brazilian Amyr Klink? I remember him saying something like this: ... *it's good to arrive when you have patience. To get anywhere, I learned that you don't need to master strength, but reason... you need, before anything else, to want*!

Brazilian? With that name?... I asked for the sake of asking, since it wasn't important to the conversation... but the doctor responded promptly: yes, Brazilian, Rose and from São Paulo and, in my opinion, he is a great example of patience, persistence, determination, discipline, focus, etc.

Wow, doctor... I asked... what does he do, crochet? Oh! Oh! Oh! No Rose... she laughed... what he did was something absolutely incredible... he was the only one on this planet to cross the Atlantic Ocean in a rowboat, from the city of Lüderitz, on the coast of Namibia, to the city from Salvador, Bahia. Patience, indeed, was his main instrument because, in a small boat less than 6 meters long and one and a half meters wide, he rowed for one hundred days (8 hours a day) the equivalent of almost 7 thousand kilometers. An unprecedented feat, Rose, a most eloquent example of patience and persistence!

Wow, doctor, impressive... I said... I'm even going to eat another cookie. Want more coffee? ... I asked, standing up and saying... really, without patience and persistence he wouldn't have achieved this, would he?

You're right, Rose... she said... just half a cup, please! We strayed a little from the topic of meditation, but it was important to talk about persistence and patience, which are fundamental to good meditation. Let's continue?

Yes, let's do it... I replied, returning to my chair... you can continue, doctor. She put the cup back on the table, put her hands together and started again.

The objective of meditation, Rose, is to promote an integration of the practitioner's mind and heart. It is not a complicated or essentially difficult practice. In fact, it is a strictly mental activity. While this is true, it is also not enough to define what meditation is. See... distraction is also a strictly mental activity and sometimes we use the body for this practice.

Doctor... I started asking and crossing my legs... does meditation calm your thoughts? Look Rose... she replied... meditation has nothing to do with calming thoughts, much less eliminating them, as many people insist on thinking. In fact, meditation helps organize thoughts, bringing them into order, focus and helping to bring clarity between them. This is how you get better answers to any questions.

You know what I would like, doctor... I interrupted... a step-by-step recipe on how to meditate. Can I do it alone without someone to guide me? Of course you can, Rose... she said... in fact there are a series of apps that help with meditation, there are videos on the internet... but I'm going to give you some tips now.

Take a moment for yourself!

Throughout the day, take a moment to disconnect from everything and connect with yourself. This is very important! It could be in the morning, after waking up and drinking coffee; it could be in the middle of the day; or before going to bed. The ideal is a period of 10 to 15 minutes to start seeing small benefits, especially in relation to breathing... in the first 5 minutes you will already feel a sense of tranquility.

Find a calm place!

It has to be a place where you can sit calmly, like a living room, a garden, a sofa or even your chair here in the office.

Choose a comfortable posture!

Rose... forget that posture we see around... of the person sitting in the lotus position. In fact, this position requires some training and, for those just starting out, it can be very uncomfortable. For you, it's better to meditate sitting down. Want to see? Grab that chair and sit down.

Can't it be here in the armchair?... I asked with a silly laugh... it's so good here! Yes it can... she replied... but this is a didactic moment and there is always more availability of a chair than an armchair, right?

Okay, doctor... I said, getting up and sitting in the chair.

It's not necessary to do it now, but before you sit down and meditate, it's a good idea to do some stretches, ok? Feel that your feet are firmly on the floor. Now place your hands on your legs... that's it! Keep your chin slightly raised. You're a little bent over, Rose... make sure your spine is always straight, without forcing it. The important thing is that you achieve a posture that allows you to remain relaxed and, at the same time, awake and attentive.

Pay attention to breathing!

Another important thing, Rose, is your breathing. You have to pay special attention to your breathing, using your lungs fully. You must inhale deeply, drawing in air to inflate your belly and chest. Then exhale slowly and pleasantly.

Exhaling is releasing the air, right?... I asked. The doctor kind of laughed without opening her mouth, certainly unsure whether I was serious or joking.

Controlling your breathing, Rose, may not be easy at first, but it is important that it is comfortable and without forcing. A cool tip is to mentally count to 4 while inhaling and then do the same thing while exhaling.

I did what she said and... wow, doctor, I got a little dizzy! Of course, Rose, you breathed in and out very quickly. This has to be done slowly so that it is pleasant and not a bad experience. Are you anxious, thinking about something? Or someone? (She made a naughty expression).

My God... I thought... did it really look that obvious? But I didn't tell her anything about Percy... of course I was thinking about him! But does she hear thoughts? As far as I know, she is a psychoanalyst and not a mentalist. Geez.

Thinking about someone?... I asked, pretending to be a fool... no way, doctor! At the moment there is no itch to scratch! Not me, gross! She then delicately took a cookie and sat down in the armchair. She took the cookie to her mouth but didn't bite. She just touched it lightly to her lips and, with a silly smile and an oblique look, she asked me: What's your Portuguese teacher like? Percy, right?

Jesus, Mary, Joseph, and the entire apostolate... the doctor is a witch! I felt like someone had reached into my mouth, pulled out my intestines and wrapped it around my neck. How...how did you...how did you know, doctor?... I asked, completely disconcerted.

Rose, dear... she said, biting the cookie... when you were outside with Nair, I was flipping through your Portuguese module. I got it like that... just to get it... I like this subject! Then I saw that you wrote the name Percy on the back cover, in whimsically round letters decorated with lots of little hearts. I thought to myself: Wow... Rose is dragging her heels for someone! Are you or are you not?... she asked with a sharp, penetrating look and a welcoming smile with sealed lips.

Yes... I am, doctor!... I replied a little embarrassed... I mean, I think I am! It's nothing serious... he doesn't even know I exist in that class, nor does he pay me any special attention. It's just in my head! Don't worry!

Worried? Me???... she exclaimed laughing... Look, Rose... I'm going to tell you the same thing you told Nair. Because she told me about your conversation and that you told her, rightly, to prioritize her brain and not pay attention to her heart! Well, do that too, Rose! And meditation can help you a lot... because with it you will be the protagonist of your thoughts and not a supporting player, understand? There's no need to be shy... we are women, and we must help each other. Trust me, okay? Shall we resume our conversation about meditation? Let's do it, doctor... I replied, now more confident... let's get to the point!

At that moment I felt that Percy was much smaller in my head. Better this way, I thought. Very good, Rose... she started again... there was still one more tip left for you who are going to start practicing meditation.

Focus and concentration!

When we talk about traditional meditation, we are talking about finding a focus to maintain attention. We can generally use a mantra, which can be any sound, a syllable, word, or phrase, which must be repeated several times to exert a specific power over your mind and which will help you concentrate for the meditation.

When she said "mantra", I immediately wanted to make puns. I thought, but I didn't say: Mantra, whoever can, obeys whoever has sense! Hmmm... not bad! Ten out of ten for puns, but for concentration and focus... zero! Doctor... so mantra could be a sentence?... I asked, trying to regain concentration...

Of course you can, Rose... would you already have one? Yes... I replied... I remember when I was a girl, every morning my father heard a guy say on the radio: Every day, from every point of view, I get better and better! I spent my childhood hearing this. I think this phrase "I'm going to get better and better" is a good mantra. What do you think?

Well, I think it's very good! By the way, Rose, words have power! So much so that mantras have been chanted for millennia... more than the repetition of words, the vibrations produced by mantras release endorphins, aligning our thoughts, increasing our focus, and preventing our mind from thinking about several things at the same time. This is what we call the auditory method!

But there is also the visual method!... she continued... In general, contemplation is, let's say, looking with admiration and also more attention. In an art gallery, for example, when we look at a painting that caught our attention, we are actually more than simply looking... we are admiring it. At that moment, our entire mind is focused on the beauty of that work.

But doctor... I started by asking... besides a work of art, it could be something else, right? It's so hard to go to a gallery... in fact I don't even know where they are! No, no, Rose... she corrected... the work of art was just an example. It can also be a beautiful landscape, the movement of the waters of a river, the waves of the sea... this visual meditation practice makes you integrate with what is being contemplated. You become that object and that object becomes you. When you manage to reach this "mixture", it means that you have achieved your goal of calming and organizing your thoughts.

Doctor... I asked... at first it must be difficult to keep your mind focused only on what we are contemplating, right? Well, Rose... it is very common for different thoughts to arise during meditation. In this case, you shouldn't "fight" with them. Just let them come and then leave. Over time and with practice, it becomes easier not to get caught up in your thoughts.

Did you understand so far, Rose?... asked the doctor, offering me a cookie. As I never reject anything, I accepted, of course! Doctor... I asked again... what is the biggest benefit of meditation?

Wow, Rose... she replied... there are so many. There are countless health benefits, which is why it has been increasingly practiced. This, with the great advantage that you can practice most of the exercises anywhere and at any time, without the need to invest in equipment.

Good thing, doctor... I joked... at the moment I don't even have the cash to buy a band-aid! Oh! Oh! Oh! Oh, Rose... she said, laughing a lot... I almost choked on my coffee. But let's go to the benefits of meditation. I've already talked about some, but let's go to the main ones. Look:

- Relax the mind.
- Restores health.
- Helps with concentration.
- Reduces anxiety.
- Reduces stress and irritability.
- Increases creativity.
- Improves memorization.
- Increases productivity.
- Regulates mood changes.
- Regulates sleep pattern.

Is it good or do you want more?... asked the doctor laughing... but there are more benefits, Rose, that result from good meditation but there are also some challenges.

Challenges?... I asked in amazement... what do you mean challenges? Well, Rose... she replied... meditation can be practiced by most people, but it can be a challenge for others. People who have, for example, attention deficit disorder will have extremely impaired concentration. This is because this disorder blocks the person's ability to concentrate.

Is this thing a disease, doctor?... I asked... Yes, dear, it's a chronic illness... the person has difficulty paying attention, hyperactivity, and impulsivity. We call this disease ADHD, that is, attention deficit hyperactivity disorder, which can begin in childhood and continue into adulthood.

So, doctor... (another cookie) ... the person who has this...suffers what? Well, Rose... she said... the person has low self-esteem, problematic relationships and difficulty studying or working. But don't worry... you don't have any of that!... she added, smiling.

Good thing, doctor... I exclaimed... although I have difficulty with some subjects. I can't pay attention or concentrate when it comes to Mathematics, Physics, Chemistry... but I do well in History, Geography and... Portuguese!

Mainly in Portuguese, right Rose?... she joked... in this subject the attention and concentration is total, right? It's true... I replied, blushing... but is there a difference between attention and concentration?

Yes, there is... she said... concentration is the ability to stay focused on what you are doing. With attention, you notice the details and nuances of what is being done. In Portuguese classes, for example, you focus on the subject, while Percy explains the lessons on the board. And you probably pay close attention to the way he dresses, talks... etc.

Didn't I say it?... I thought to myself... this doctor is a witch. It must be!

So, Rose... she asked, cutting off my thoughts... when are you going to start meditating? Don't give me the "I'll start on Monday" story! I already know that story!

Oh! Oh! Ah!... I laughed... you are terrible! Geez!

I say this, Rose... she said, explaining herself... because beginners in meditation always have excuses that prevent them from taking the first step, such as: lack of time, very agitated mind, physical discomfort, boredom, sleepiness... These people always want immediate results, which don't always happen.

In my opinion, Rose... she continued... there are two major obstacles for those just starting out: numbness and drowsiness. In numbness, the mind is sluggish and heavy, and if you don't react to this, the numbness causes a feeling of complete sleep. Drowsiness is when we feel sleepy during the day or have prolonged sleep at night.

Doctor... I interrupted... I feel very drowsy when I read a lot or when I'm on the subway or bus. Wow... I take a few naps, and someone always comes to wake me up when I have to get off.

It's just that when you doze off, Rose... you don't sleep, but you lose attention and, with that, you lose the means of waking up. But I'm going to give you a tip so you don't let yourself become numb or doze off when that can't happen. It's the candle in the dark exercise... turn off the lights in the bedroom or living room and light a candle and watch the shadows that form on the wall. You don't need to see everything... just the ones you can decipher.

The important thing is not to see everything, but to see what is essential. Thus, concentration must rest from all secondary actions, to achieve the peace that allows you to achieve during practice. It's a great exercise to do every now and then!

Well, Rose... that's what I wanted to tell you about meditation! Did you like it?

Before answering, I sighed and looked at her with a soulful face asking for a prayer. I was tired and worried... given the time, I had already missed the first class. Which was great, since the first class was with Mr. Potato Head. But the second class, I didn't want to miss it at all... I told her that and she gave me a mischievous smile.

Okay, Rose... just to close, I want you to remember the three important pillars of meditation: first, **breathing**... any meditation practice involves being absolutely aware of your breathing. Second, **concentration**... choose the object of meditation, something to focus on and concentrate on. Third and last, **self-knowledge**, meditating is also self-observing, looking inside. Okay, Rose? Now go so you don't miss class...

Oh, doctor, thank you... I said, standing up... today was great.

Yes... she said with a wink... and so will the night. Regards to Percy... she added, laughing.

Ah, doctor... I exclaimed... this story will still give you a lot of meditation!

I hope so... she said, taking the bag of cookies... take some cookies.

I did like Nair... I grabbed a handful and went a mile a minute! The doctor was laughing!

CHAPTER 9

Emotional Intelligence

So... these days I was thinking about Nair and her radical change. I confess that I felt a little envious... a good kind of envy, of course! Not just because she is prettier, more attractive... (although she is still a little overweight). But mainly, because she has become a resolute, determined woman who knows her worth.

Well, actually my "envy" kind of doesn't make sense. I also think I'm resolved, determined, and know my own worth. But I don't know, I'm missing something. I also think I'm too suspicious to say that... yes, I'm beautiful and attractive. But I think I am... because sometimes, at school, I feel guys looking at me. It's true that it's that kind of look, like someone in a self-service restaurant, passing by the food and thinking "take it or don't take it...eat it or don't eat it!" And, if you're really hungry, grab and eat anything!

Ah, but when it comes to that, I'm a tough woman... whoever tries to be slick, I tell them "Get over it" right away! My disastrous marriage left me a little wary about men. Now I'm like a dog bitten by a snake... it even gets smart when it finds a sausage.

In class I have a reputation for being picky. The guys already know that with me they can't just... "come over"! But I'm not the unfriendly type. I treat everyone well, I respond politely when they ask me something, sometimes I make a joke during a class that even provokes laughter but that's it. I never leave the slightest impression that "I am available".

The only person I have a little more conversation with is Alaor, a bachelor who has a huge crush on Pituca, the science teacher. He's a good guy... tall without a belly, brown eyes, blonde hair that's a bit curly, an open and frank smile and he laughs a lot at my jokes. We get along very well! When I met him, on the first few days of school, the guy caught my attention. I even gave him my look 42, which presupposes curiosity and some sexual speculation.

But, when we spoke for the first time, I discovered a serious problem with Alaor, which made me immediately "pull the handbrake": bad breath! This was on the first day of school after we sat at our desks next to each other. He turned to me and asked if, like him, I was also going back to school. At the time, I wanted to ask what he had eaten before coming to school... a crow sandwich? But I kept to myself and, discreetly, looked ahead, out of the line of his breath. I don't remember what I answered... I just know that nowadays, when we talk, I kind of disguise it, turn away, etc. The problem is that you can't go up to the guy and talk about this problem. Like: "Listen… could you get a mint candy?" or maybe... "Sorry... I left beans on the stove. Keep talking and I'll be right back!" I can't... I can't! It's very embarrassing!

Another thing... he dresses really badly! One day those jeans of his are going to come to school on their own. It's so greasy that he certainly doesn't put it in his closet. I think he leaves it standing in the corner. When it's time to use it, he doesn't put it on... he jumps in! The other day he came with a t-shirt full of holes. It gave the impression that he was putting his t-shirt out to dry in the moth laundry.

Anyway... Alaor is just a friend and, even so, from a distance! Even because, lately, the one who has been throwing me off balance is him, Percy, the Portuguese teacher... not tall, not short, brown eyes, slightly brownish hair with a hint of gray (I think he highlights it). He has clear, clean skin and a suggestive nose and I wonder what a suggestive nose would be? I don't know... but it's an intimidating nose. His beard is always unshaven, which gives him a certain charm of, let's say, shabby chic. He has big hands, which wield the marker on the blackboard with vigor... even his handwriting impresses me.

Anyway, in his classes I keep traveling between pronouns, adverbs, conjunctions... and, at the same time, I get carried away by the tone of his voice, by his walk around the room explaining the material. When he passes through my desk, it leaves an almost imperceptible trail of delicious cologne. I even think he was born with that smell... like the Adam's apple, which is born with us. If only he would notice me... just a little. Then the questions come: is he married, engaged?

Well, he doesn't have a ring... although that doesn't mean anything nowadays. Maybe he has a friend with benefits. I don't know... all I can say is that I, damn it, am completely in love with him from head to toe...

These days I mentioned this acute crush of mine to the doctor. She told me something about emotional intelligence, which I've heard about, but I don't really know what it is. I think it's something about using emotions intelligently... I don't know, I think that's it. Isn't it?

Your thinking is in the right direction, Rose... she told me, taking a sip of her coffee. The last patient of the day had already left, and we were in her office talking. Rose... she said, putting the cup back on the saucer... it almost feels like you're telling me something new. You think I didn't notice your eyes getting bright when you told me about this Portuguese teacher... Percy, right?

That's right, doctor... I replied a little shyly and embarrassed. I mean, a bit of a senseless shame, because Dr. Norma exudes confidence and it's only with her that I could open up. I said everything I was feeling. How much Percy was messing with my head, disturbing me, filling me with dreams, etc., etc. I asked how much this emotional intelligence could help me.

Rose... she began... before we talk about Percy, let's talk about emotional intelligence, which is one of the main factors in dealing with problems of, as you say, acute crush!

Emotional intelligence, Rose, is something that is very much in evidence these days. I don't know if you've heard anything about it, but you certainly don't know how much emotional intelligence can impact your goals... be they personal or professional.

At the moment... I thought but didn't say... my goals are more emotional.

To begin to understand this subject, Rose... she continued... I'm going to use a classic example about what happens when emotional intelligence is lacking. See... many people are hired by a company because of their technical skills. But they are often fired because of their behavior.

Does this really happen, doctor? I asked. I mean, it doesn't matter if the person is a beast at what they do, but takes the fall for bad behavior?

Exactly, Rose... and this has been the criterion of large organizations over the last few decades. See... more and more technical aspects are undergoing the most incredible technological advances, such as artificial intelligence, for example. But, on the other hand, the requirement for behavioral skills has also increased, that is, it is not enough to be a tremendous technician when dealing with machines. The person also has to be skilled in dealing with people. Have the flexibility to resolve complex situations that arise between your subordinates and, of course, your superiors.

I understand, doctor... I interrupted... in a company, defects or problems don't only occur with the machines, right? Problems can also happen with people...

That's right, Rose... she replied... this is when the emotional intelligence of a person who has the aptitude to deal with the most varied situations of conflict between employees, dealing with emotions, and challenging day-to-day situations comes into play.

Wow, doctor... I said... that means that emotional intelligence ends up having nothing to do with technical capacity but, rather, with the ability to deal with... with... I'm missing the word... .

... with social relationships, Rose, social and personal given the circumstances. Oh, yes, doctor... that's exactly what I was going to say... I lied through my teeth. She laughed. It's okay, Rose... she said, taking the cup... I know you understand!

Doctor... I asked... is a person born with emotional intelligence? Because I honestly...

Well, Rose... until recently this was a question among scholars. But today we know that is not the case. Emotional intelligence not only can but should be developed by each person, regardless of their cultural level, purchasing power, religious orientation... in short, anyone can be emotionally intelligent as long as, of course, they dedicate themselves to it.

Wow, doctor, do you mean I can also be emotionally intelligent? Can you imagine? Don't you think I could even win over Percy?

Well Rose... she said with a condescending air... whether he will fall in love with you is another story. Because the terrain of love is very swampy, and we never know when we will step on solid ground or when we will sink. But you'll certainly stand out in your relationships in class... and, who knows, he'll start to notice you.

I understand... I said, lowering my head. The doctor's response was a bit of a cold shower. She noticed my disappointment and offered me coffee, saying: Rose, dear... any relationship, whether in the beginning, in the middle or at the end, can be challenging and complicated. This includes friendships between you and people in your class. But in the case of your crush on your teacher, we are talking about love. Look... this little word, love, with just four letters represents a kind of human engine. But we also know, it's a feeling that can cause a lot of headaches. I remember a (Brazilian) country song that was very successful... what was it again, Rose? It said something like this... (and she hummed) *É o amoooor* (It's love) ... what was it like, Rose? Do you remember?

Of course, I remembered it right away (bless Percy!). I looked at her, cleared my throat (blessed cigarette) and sang: *É o amor... que mexe com a minha cabeça e me deixa assim! Que faz eu pensar em você e esquecer de mim...!* (It's love... that messes with my head and leaves me like this! That makes me think about you and forget about myself...!)

Oh! Oh! Oh! Rose... that's right! Hey! You sing kind of well... she joked. Oh no, doctor... I replied... the last time I went to karaoke, I started singing a song that required really high pitches... wow, what a shame! People didn't know if someone was singing or if they were bleeding a boar... Geez. Never again!

She had cackled! Oh, Rose... only you to make me laugh! Look... did you pay attention to a detail in this part of the lyrics? What is it again? "That makes me think about you and forget about myself...". That's right... I agreed. Well then... she said... not forgetting yourself is one of the main factors that can help you avoid turning your passion into a tsunami of emotions. But see... just as important as not forgetting yourself is knowing yourself well and learning to manage your own emotions well.

I made a confused expression. This was all very new to me. The doctor noticed it right away. Rose... she said... it seems complicated, but it's not.

But doctor... I asked... after all, what is managing emotions?

Rose... she said, pouring more coffee... managing emotions is nothing more than the ability that some people have to better understand their feelings and emotions. This way they are able to act in a more calculated and reasonable way, without letting themselves be carried away by negative impulses and thoughts or influences. Do you understand?

Got it... but doctor, aren't feelings and emotions from the same bag? No, dear... she said laughing and almost choking on her coffee because of the colloquial sincerity of my question.

In fact, Rose... replied, putting the cup back on the saucer... they are from different bags! Oh! Oh! Oh! This time it was me who laughed... but what is the difference between feeling and emotion, doctor?

You see... she replied... feelings belong to the person themselves and only they know about them. Emotions can be observed by others. See... emotions are a reaction to the stimuli you receive, like watching a film that impresses you, for example. Or, suddenly, seeing

Professor Percy enter the classroom... (she smiled). Feelings are independent.

When talking about Percy, she didn't notice my heart beating fast, as if it were in a drum circle. In fact, Rose... she continued... it is emotions that give rise to feelings. As I said, emotions are an instinctive reaction, a response to external stimuli such as crying and laughter. Feelings, in general, just reflect how we feel about an emotion.

Would you like a cookie, doctor? I interrupted, pouring myself another cup of coffee... are we already talking about emotional intelligence? Well, Rose... she said, taking the cookie... everything I've told you so far is just the basics when it comes to emotional intelligence. Let's say... a kickoff!

We ate the cookie with coffee, and she looked at the clock saying... Wow, it's about to be 6 o'clock! This cookie made me hungry! Do you have important classes today? Not really, doctor... I answered, finding the question strange... because after the first two classes, Geography and Physics, there will be a lecture on social networks and education. Important, but a bummer! But why do you ask?

Rose... she said, getting up... I have an idea! Today is Friday, we don't work tomorrow, you only have two classes and none of them are Percy's, right? Right... I replied, frowning... but why do you ask? I insisted. Rose... she confessed... I could stay talking to you until midnight, but I am hungry, and I would like to go home and have dinner. So, I thought... why not invite you home with me. What do you think? While I prepare dinner for us, we continue our conversation about emotional intelligence. We can even, perhaps, order Chinese food. Do you like that?

Wow, doctor... I could trade a kidney for some orange chicken, but it's not even funny how broke I am. No, Rose... she said, taking her coat and bag... don't worry! Today you are my guest!

Wow, it's going to be a pleasure... I said, accepting the invitation. Especially because at home I would have to make good old chicken noodle soup. I just said I was worried about the timing to go home. But she reassured me by saying that she would drive me to the subway station. Perfect! We just picked up our things, closed the office and off we went.

✱✱✱✱✱✱✱✱✱✱✱✱✱✱✱✱✱✱✱✱✱✱✱

The first thing that caught my attention about Dr. Norma's house was its elegance. A single-story house with a large driveway with a small garden and parking in front. Beautiful house! I've heard that a house and the interior decoration say a lot about who lives there.

You can come in, Rose... she said, placing the keys on a sideboard... I'm just going to my room to hang up this blouse and put on some slippers. Make yourself at home, okay?

I sat on the huge couch and looked around, amazed! Right in front of me, a multi-inch television. The living room, combined with the kitchen, in fact, has the doctor's aesthetic... everything is very beautiful, but without ostentation. A marble counter separates the two spaces and creates an intelligent mix of elegance and simplicity. On the left side of the counter, a screen hides what I think is a modest bookstand. Everywhere, without exaggeration, trinkets and decorations; on the walls, small paintings with optimistic phrases... all showing the doctor's mystical side.

Ready, Rose! she said, returning... I took the opportunity to take off my "doctor" uniform. At home, of course, I'm more comfortable in sweatshirts and a t-shirt. Shall we call the restaurant? she asked, taking out her cell phone... let's see, for you an order of orange chicken and for me chicken in ginger sauce. I'll also order a portion of spring rolls. To drink, there is orange juice in the fridge.

While she called, I got up and sat on one of the stools at the marble counter, where we would probably eat, and continued to observe the room. Everything arranged with great care and distinction. In other words, just like the doctor!

Okay, Rose... she said... they said it would arrive in half an hour. Let's sit here on the couch and talk. Come, Rose... I told you, make yourself at home! I sat down, already really feeling at ease. Suddenly the doctor looked at a long tube next to the television, saying: Alexa... play music for reflection and this Alexa said something that I didn't understand and then started playing soft, delicious music.

Did you know Alexa, Rose? she asked, noticing my look of surprise. I had already heard of it, doctor... I responded... but we were never introduced. That's awesome! Well, Rose... she said without ostentation... Alexa is one of the results of artificial intelligence and for me, who lives alone, she is a good companion and a virtual assistant. It simplifies my life, answering everything I ask for, such as the time, day of the week, weather forecast, news, turning the lights on and off in the room... in addition, of course, to playing any music I want to hear.

Incredible, doctor... I said, already starting a little joke... if I ask her for some toasted bread with butter, will she, do it? Or make Percy interested in me, can she find a way? Oh! Oh! Ah!... the doctor said, laughing... no Rose, Alexa is an artificial intelligence and not a chef, nor an emotional intelligence.

Damn, not everything is perfect... I said, making a sigh of discontent. She laughed and said that, with regards to Percy, whatever will be will be and that I shouldn't worry. From time to time.

Meanwhile, Rose... she continued... try to understand yourself better, because the first step towards developing your emotional intelligence is self-knowledge. In fact, this is a continuous process, which never ends.

All the time? I asked, thinking seriously not only about Percy, but also about the orange chicken that was about to arrive. Hunger was already getting angry... because my large intestine was already starting to eat the small one.

Yes, dear... she replied... throughout our lives we are evolving, growing spiritually. Little by little we expand our awareness and, as a result, we change over time. This, of course, requires a constant and continuous process of self-knowledge.

Got it... doctor, I interrupted... but what do I really need to know about myself? Well, Rose... she replied... in the development of emotional intelligence it is essential that you learn to recognize your emotions and what caused those emotions. See... each person has a different emotional reaction when a trigger is pressed, such as good or bad news, an impactful film, etc.

You Rose... she said looking into my eyes... how do you react when you feel a very strong negative emotion? Or how do you react when the emotion is positive?

Ah, doctor... I replied... if it's a negative emotion of anger, I'll let out some heavy swear words. But if it's sadness, sometimes I can't hold back some tears. But in positive emotions I react with euphoria and contentment. Normal, right?

Yes, Rose... all these emotions are part of our daily lives and behind them are our thoughts about the things that were linked to these emotions. I'll give you an example... she continued... let's suppose Percy invites you to dinner. It's just a hypothesis, okay? Right... a hypothesis! I replied, but inside I desperately wanted it to happen one day. In seconds I could see myself with him in a fancy restaurant, with candlelight, having a drink, the kind with an umbrella, him looking at me with those brown eyes, looking like he was going to tell me...

... I'm sorry, but I can't do it anymore today... the doctor continued with her hypothesis... he says to you on the phone. How would you react, Rose? How would I react, doctor? One of two things: either I would release the dogs on him, or I would look for the first overpass that was very high. I would die of hatred!

Well then, Rose (laughs)... perhaps the emotion you experience is one of deep frustration transformed into anger. After all, you may have created expectations, right? It may also be that you feel insecure for fear that, in reality, he has given up because he is not very interested in you. Well, doctor... I interrupted... in this case I hope it's a very high overpass.

She laughed, saying: only you, Rose! But do you realize that emotions, whether positive or negative, provoke immediate rationalizations? In your case, due to uncontrolled anger, you began to think dysfunctionally, that is, in an irrational way that can lead to harmful behaviors. I wouldn't want to be in that teacher's place.

I ended up laughing too. But doctor... I asked... what if he canceled dinner because of an important unforeseen event? Which I would only accept in cases of open fracture or family mourning. She had to laugh again. Look Rose... she pondered... an unforeseen event, whatever it may be, doesn't necessarily mean that that person was no longer interested in you. But let's say he just says it's an important unforeseen event but doesn't say what it is. I believe that the strong emotion of frustration, followed by anger, will make you behave irrationally in the same way. There will be unwanted reactions that will bring negative consequences.

So, what to do, doctor... I asked, a little distressed, living in that situation... it's the million-dollar question! Rose, look... she explained... when you are under the influence of a strong emotion, negative or positive, never take immediate action. Stop, sit, relax, count to ten and wait for the emotion to decrease in intensity. The ancients always said that time is the best medicine!

And then, doctor?... I asked. Well, Rose, by doing this you will have time to think better about that fateful phone call, you will clarify your thoughts and, thus, you will make the right decisions. In other words, at the first opportunity you will meet the professor, who will explain better why he canceled dinner.

At that moment the doorbell rang. Speaking of dinner, it must be the food... she said... getting up to answer the door. Yay!!! I thought but didn't say it, after all I also have some pedigree. I just made a soft expression of someone who was almost eating the doctor's couch cushion.

Look how beautiful this is, Rose... she said, smiling and walking quickly towards the counter, in a kind of childish gluttony. I liked seeing this moment that I would say belonged to Norma and not the doctor. I got up from the couch and went to help her tidy up the food. It smelled great! She pointed me to a drawer in a small piece of furniture so I could get two placemats to support the plates, cutlery and napkin.

We sat down to eat and, I confess, it's been a long time since I had dinner with such good and delicious food and in such good company. During dinner I told the doctor about her house... so clean, so in order, nothing out of place. Rose... she explained... I like an organized house. In fact, it is a personal exercise that requires self-knowledge. Well, in this aspect I know myself a lot and I know that a messy house will impact my mental health. So, I'm very attentive to this... but without being a perfectionist! I watch myself a lot, because perfectionism also brings negative feelings.

But are you the one in charge of cleaning the house? I asked, although I couldn't see the doctor in the headscarf wielding a mop or operating a vacuum cleaner. Rose... she replied... I love cleaning! But I pay a girl who, every Friday, comes to do a deeper cleaning of the house. You know, I even help her... more out of pleasure than out of necessity. Look Rose... nothing better than a good cleaning to clear your mind and soul! Do you agree? How can I disagree with her?... I thought... Impossible!

We finished dinner and she got up saying she was going to make us some tea. Green Tea... she told me... that helps digestion. Easterners know their stuff! Ah, Rose... after tea, if you want to smoke, there's a bench in my garden. Sit there and smoke your cigarette in peace, while I take care of these dishes.

I didn't think twice because, after the tea, the desire to smoke came like the aroma of a barbecue in a refugee's nose. You really don't mind, doctor?... I asked. Of course not, Rose... she replied... I just don't like people smoking in the house. There's even an ashtray there, because I sometimes have friends over who smoke. Go on, Rose... don't worry! On the way back we'll continue our conversation.

After the cigarette, I went back inside, and everything was impeccable again. The doctor was already on the sofa finishing another cup of tea. I sat down and started asking a question. Doctor... I started... is it possible for us to control our emotions? I mean... faced with a situation that will make me good or bad, is it possible for me to avoid feeling the emotions that will be caused by that situation?

Good question, Rose... she said, placing the cup on the saucer... no, it's not possible! You cannot control your emotions, but rather your reaction to them. Wanting to avoid an emotion would be like wanting to stop your digestive functions or stop your bloodstream. It's impossible!

This is because it is human nature to feel emotions and we do not have the option not to feel them. Even though it is a very strong emotion, you cannot cancel it and, at your pleasure, stop feeling it.

Like a car without brakes going downhill... I interrupted... you have to hold the steering wheel, call all the saints, let it crash and see what happens.

More or less that, Rose... she said laughing... but that would be a negative emotion, right? The same happens when the emotion is positive, for example, discovering that Percy has been speaking highly of you in the staff room. You can't decide not to feel this emotion either. Now, when these emotions happen, the only thing you can do, or rather, the only power you have is in how you will react to these emotions. How would you react, Rose?

I don't know, doctor... I replied... in the case of the car without brakes, I think I would get wrecked, and I wouldn't even be awake to feel any emotion. Of course, after being admitted, I would have to react with resignation and patience. But if Percy spoke well of me in the staff room, I would react... I would react... I don't know, doctor, I would die of curiosity. What did he say and to whom?

It doesn't matter, Rose... she said... the first thing to do is accept this emotion. That's right! Resisting the emotions that assault us only makes everything intensify and worse: it doesn't change anything! Same thing if you sweep your house and push the trash under the rug. The house will look clean, but the trash will still be there, under the rug. In other words, emotions, whether negative or positive, will continue to pulse within you.

I got it doctor... I questioned... but I still haven't connected one thing to the other. Emotions, emotional intelligence...

Rose... she said... I think I told you when we were in my office, that emotional intelligence is nothing more than knowing how to manage your emotions, you must have forgotten. But it does not matter! Emotional intelligence is the ability to identify and deal with personal and other individuals' emotions and feelings.

Ah, I remember, doctor... I interrupted... you said that in emotional intelligence it is essential that we learn to deal with emotions. Right?

That's right, dear... she exclaimed with satisfaction... for example: a person who is sad and anxious for some reason. Even though they have these bad feelings, they manage, throughout the day, to do a good job, finish their tasks and achieve their goals.

Got it... I said... they just didn't let the problems interfere with their work. Exactly, Rose... the doctor agreed... they were skilled enough to manage their feelings better.

Who invented this emotional intelligence thing, doctor? Well, Rose... there are several references to important authors who dealt with this subject and contributed to arriving at the current definition of emotional intelligence.

But nothing compares to the fantastic work of science journalist Daniel Goleman (she took out her cell phone and typed quickly). Look, Rose, his photo... he is also a psychologist, a renowned writer... known all over the world.

He's handsome... I said, giving her the cell phone back... reminded me of Percy. Rose, Rose... she exclaimed with a condescending air... the way you're in love you'll see this Percy in a radish.

We both burst into laughter. Wow, doctor... radish? Just kidding, Rose... she said, typing again on her cell phone... but look, this was the book he wrote – Emotional Intelligence -, in 1995, which was fundamental for studying this subject. To give you an idea, this book sold around 5 million copies and was translated into almost 50 countries. I think I have a copy in my office. Pick it up on Monday and start reading it... you'll like it, and it will help you a lot.

But isn't it complicated?... I asked... isn't it a very technical language? On the contrary... she replied... he uses language that is very accessible to the general public, very easy to understand. But regardless, let's continue our conversation.

Okay, doctor... Monday I'll start reading. I really want to start dealing better with my emotions. That's right, Rose... in fact, a person's ability to deal with their emotions is much more important than their competence in dealing with technical data or processing information. Look how incredible... you must have heard of something called IQ, right?

Right... I replied... it has to do with intelligence, right? Yes... she replied... is the acronym for Intelligence Quotient. Well then, Daniel Goleman invented something parallel called EQ, that is, Emotional Quotient. He says that 80% of a person's success has to do with their EQ. IQ is responsible for the other 20%. Did you realize the importance of knowing how to work with emotions?

Wow, doctor... I exclaimed... impressive! This means that there's no point in someone having an IQ on the top floor, but when it comes to resolving an emotional situation, they fail! Geez!

True, Rose... she said, laughing... it's no surprise that Goleman conceptualizes emotional intelligence as being the ability to manage feelings, so that they contribute to good decision-making.

Look Rose... I'll tell you something. For a long time, the only way we had to measure someone's intelligence was through the Intelligence Quotient.

So, what is IQ if not the ability to reason? Is it not true? In other words, thinking about problems abstractly, generating solutions to complex subjects and learning quickly.

So that means, doctor... I asked... that emotional intelligence is also something to be mastered? Of course, Rose... and mastering emotional intelligence means being able to perceive your emotions, knowing how to name them, understanding what caused them and then developing ways to deal with them.

Doctor... I'm curious... how many emotions do we have. Someone already counted them... if it's a stupid question, I'm sorry! No, Rose... she replied, laughing... it's not a stupid question! Know that some studies talk about 27 emotions and others already talk about almost 50 different emotions including happiness, anger, anguish, relief, boredom and so on!

In fact, Rose... she continued... being aware of the emotions we experience from time to time allows us to understand the reasons that caused them. From there, it will be possible to develop ways to deal with them. As time passes, Rose, you will realize that you have more flexibility to deal with your emotions. You will feel that you are becoming a lighter, more optimistic person and that solving emotional problems is no longer a burden.

So, doctor... I asked... when I know how to control my emotions, know everything about them, does that mean I'm emotionally intelligent? Without a doubt, dear... she replied... at that moment you will have control over your emotional intelligence.

CHAPTER 10
The Pillars of Emotional Intelligence

Do you know what would be interesting now, Rose? Another cup of tea?... I joked... that would be a good idea! Also, Rose... grab a thermos and bring me one too... she said, handing me her cup. But what I want to say is that it would be interesting for us to do, now, a kind of step-by-step guide for you to start developing your emotional intelligence.

Let's do it, doctor... I said, bringing the cups of tea. What's the first step?

<u>Knowing your emotions</u>
The first thing is self-awareness, that is, your ability to understand how emotions work. How they arise, where they come from and how they manifest themselves.

But how will I know that doctor?

Rose... feelings normally provoke two types of reactions: psychological and physical. Psychological reactions concern a person's thoughts and beliefs. Physical reactions include symptoms of chills, tachycardia, for example.

When Percy passes by my desk, I smell that perfume... wow, my heart starts racing...

So... she said... this is a physical reaction, and this beating of your heart may not be a bad feeling, it's love!

An emotion such as anguish can awaken negative thoughts that make the person feel incapable and even have a physical manifestation, such as palpitations, pain in the abdomen, etc...

Control your emotions

Controlling emotions has to do with self-regulation of emotions, that is, the ability to manage your feelings.

You know, doctor... I said... I think that expression "manage" is strange. I always remember the manager of the bank where I have an account... he keeps looking at my ass! Pervert!

Okay, Rose... she said laughing... then switch to directing or even controlling your feelings. So... she continued... once you can recognize what you feel, it becomes easier to control these different sensations.

Let's suppose, Rose, that you always feel anguish in certain situations in your daily life, which will generate those physical and psychological manifestations that I already mentioned. To start identifying this bad feeling, the first step is to identify what circumstances brought it to light.

And how can I do that, doctor? I asked sipping my second tea. Well, Rose... there are two useful strategies, such as talking to yourself or keeping a personal diary.

Oh, doctor... I interrupted... I'm not sure I can handle talking to myself. I think I'll keep the diary.

She laughed a little, explaining that the idea is to always remember that I have a choice, that control of my emotions is in my hands.

Develop self-motivation

Another important thing, Rose, is to motivate yourself and stay alert to stay that way. To do this, use emotions to your advantage... towards a specific objective, be it personal or professional.

I will give you an example that you will like. Your big goal at the moment is to win over the Portuguese teacher, right? That's right, doctor... but here's the thing: if he, at some point, becomes really interested in me, that's great. Let's go. Otherwise, excuse me while the line moves! Geez.

Oh! oh! Oh! This is the Rose that I learned to know! But we're still in the field of examples, okay? In the case of winning over the teacher, it is a personal objective. But there are also professional goals, such as, for example, graduating in Psychology and, later, becoming my partner. What do you think?

Wow... I exclaimed... that would be incredible, doctor! But not impossible, she added. But in both personal and professional goals, the exercise you should do is always ask yourself: how can I control my feelings, in order to always make the best decision?

In both cases, the important thing is always to prioritize reason, because one of the keys to success lies in the balance between these two scenarios. In the case of winning over the teacher, the use of reason has to be a priority, Rose, because it is reason that will tell you that, for you, you are the most important person. Shall we move forward?

Develop empathy

If I understand the meaning of empathy, doctor... I started asking... empathy means "knowing how to put yourself in someone else's shoes", right?

That's right, Rose... she said... but it's more than that! See... besides "putting yourself in someone else's shoes", think that the other people around you, such as friends, family and co-workers or classmates, in your case... also have your emotions and you need to learn to deal with them.

I find this a bit complicated, doctor... I observed... each person has a different personality... what do you think?

Rose... she said with some gravity... perhaps the development of the emotional intelligence of all these people is lagging behind yours. Okay, in the development of emotional intelligence there is no room for judgment. Just be you, always! Now, one last thing about this.

Develop interpersonal relationships

Rose, look... no one lives alone, right? Human beings basically live from their relationships with the world. We have always needed to come together to be stronger and, together, overcome obstacles. That's what this last statement is about.

Ok, doctor... I'm all ears!

Interpersonal relationships, Rose... is another key point for success, that is, having good relationships while managing other people's emotions. This, of course, will create a positive environment around you, improving not only your quality of life, but also infecting everyone around you.

I think I'm going to have to change my behavior a little, doctor... I confessed... back in class, although I treat everyone politely, I have the reputation of being flirty. In fact, I avoid small talk that will end up resulting in a "pick-up line".

Rose, dear... the important thing is not to belittle the person and also not to belittle yourself. If they compliment you, accept and agree, showing attitude and confidence. If they ask you out and it's not in your interest, simply say no and that's it. If they insist, gently say that you already have a commitment to someone and that's it. The important thing is not to "burn" the relationship, trying to keep it on good terms.

HOW DO YOU PERCEIVE AND INTERPRET REALITY?

You know, doctor... everything you said about emotional intelligence, about controlling our emotions and everything else, I think that all of this has to do with the way we face our reality without forgetting the reality of others, right?

Exactly, Rose... she replied... and the mental attitude you take when faced with these realities or, we can say, challenges is decisive. The late American writer, Napoleon Hill, very influential on this issue of self-help, said in his works that we have two types of mental attitude: positive (PMA) and negative (NMA). This defines the way we see life, the world and the challenges that arise.

See, Rose... she continued... if you tend to see things on the positive side (PMA), more lightly, you will certainly control your emotions better. Because with positive mental attitudes you will be completely disconnected, in the long run, from negative emotions.

And the opposite, doctor... I asked... what happens?

Well... she replied... if you have a negative mental attitude (NMA), you tend to see life in a more pessimistic way, because you will always be taking the negative aspects of life into consideration. So, dear... realizing in a very frank and honest way what your mental attitude tends to be in different situations in your life is very important. This is because every day we can make the decision to think and act differently.

Now, Rose... you need to pay attention to your thoughts because there are dysfunctional automatic thoughts. Complicated little name, doctor... what is dysfunctional thought?

These are ideas, Rose... she replied... that appear in her mind automatically. They appear without "asking permission", that is, without the slightest reflection, so that the individual considers this thought as an absolute truth. Because it is dysfunctional, this thought will end up generating other thoughts just as bad as this one, which will trigger attacks of anxiety or paranoia.

Doctor... I asked... how can you tell if a thought is dysfunctional or functional? Good question, Rose... let's draw a parallel between one and the other. Look, she said, taking a notebook and a pen:

Dysfunctional Thoughts	Functional Thoughts
When you feel "stuck".	When thoughts strengthen you.
When you want to please everyone and, at the same time, want everyone's approval.	When you are consistent with your needs.
When you don't put yourself in someone else's shoes.	When you make considerations between your perception and that of the other.

When you take your thoughts as absolute truths.	When you question what you think.
When you fight your feelings.	When you understand what you think.
When you don't adapt to changes, ignoring them.	When you look for new possibilities for your development.

The important thing, Rose... is for you to understand and identify what your automatic dysfunctional thoughts are. This way, you will have a better understanding of how your mind works when facing challenges and adverse situations in life. Consequently, knowing how your mind works and being faced with a situation that provokes negative thinking, you can replace it with adaptive thinking.

Wow, doctor... what is that? Adaptive thinking... sorry, I got confused! That's normal, Rose... she replied... an adaptive thought is the one you have to replace a negative thought, allowing you to push away the negativity and focus solely on finding solutions.

I got it, doctor... I got your message... I said, making fun with my hands on my temples. You're talking about mental health, am I right? On the spot, Rose... she replied, laughing... on the spot! Do you know how to avoid dysfunctional thinking?

Hmmm... I replied... I don't know... sleeping?

Oh! Oh! Oh! Of course not, Rose! What you have to do is... first: practice meditation, we've already talked a lot about this. Second: write down negative thoughts and try to reverse them on a daily basis or share them with a psychotherapist. Third and last: try to rationalize and not get carried away by emotions.

Got it, doctor... I said, pouring myself some more tea... now, the million-dollar question. How can I put all this into practice and learn to develop emotional intelligence?

Well... she said... first, another cup of tea! Wow, doctor... I exclaimed, putting my cup on the saucer... I poured some for myself and didn't even offer it to you. Let me pour it for you.

Thank you, Rose... let me sweeten it up. You asked me how to put all these teachings into practice. So, I must start by saying that we only truly learn something when we put it into practice. At this point, it is inevitable to answer your question without mentioning challenges and opportunities.

Rose, you must remember our first conversations, when I said that our problems were, in fact, challenges that bring us opportunities for growth. Do you remember? Yes, I remember, doctor... I said, pouring myself some more tea... you even talked about seeing a problem from another angle. You also said that problems are gifts, and I was confused and asked: "Gifts?" Then you explained to me that these challenges are gifts because they are opportunities for growth and suggested that I replace the word problem with challenge. Wasn't that right?

Exactly, Rose... she said smiling... what a good memory you have! Congratulations! See how emotional intelligence is now starting to make sense. Because everyone who wants to develop emotional intelligence wants to do well when facing life's challenges. They don't want to suffer for no reason anymore, they want to have more peace of mind, happiness and lightness when facing the challenges that life offers. That's why Rose... she continued taking a sip of tea... in the challenges that arise in your life, from now on, you will have the opportunity to put these teachings into practice and improve yourself more and more.

My first challenge, doctor... I said laughing... will be to overcome the urge I have right now to smoke, after this delicious tea. Go to the garden bench, Rose... she said standing up... I'm going to take the opportunity to pee. Whenever you need to go to the bathroom it's in that hallway, first door on the left.

When I came back inside, Dr. Norma was already on the couch waiting for me. Rose... she said... I know you said it jokingly, but quitting smoking can be a big challenge, don't you think? Now you have the right tools to overcome this addiction. But look everything is a process that starts with the word acceptance. First, accept yourself... accept the idea that you are a smoker and how much harm it can do you. Only then, with acceptance, will you be able to make changes in your life.

Okay, doctor... I replied... I promise that will be my first and greatest challenge to face and... But look, Rose... she interrupted... never forget the importance of self-knowledge. Those who don't know themselves well can't set goals and end up at the mercy of circumstances, becoming frustrated.

Rose... she asked... of everything we talked about, what caught your attention the most about emotional intelligence?

Well, doctor... I tried to give an intelligent answer... I think the best deduction I can make from everything you said is that emotions are important, but so is reason. So... we have to see the heart and the brain as if they were inseparable friends. Like big and skinny, Chip and Dale, Batman and Robin...

Her laughter interrupted my answer... Oh, Rose... she said, wiping her eyes... you won't have to try very hard to be an emotionally intelligent person. Girl... you can, with intelligence and sincerity, balance the rational and the emotional, reason and intuition... logic and passion. You have an excellent Emotional Quotient!

Wow, doctor... I replied... coming from you, it's more than a compliment. It's almost like a prize. Now I just need to improve my IQ, because...

Rose... she interrupted, pointing her finger upwards... Intelligence Quotient is nothing without Emotional Quotient. What's the point of being a genius and, at the same time, being thick-skinned or a psychopath? Do you agree?

Of course, I agreed... feeling a little proud of myself. A compliment from the doctor is the best. I looked at my watch and saw that I was close to the last subway. She even suggested that I sleep there, but I didn't accept.

As promised, she took me to the subway, and I managed to catch the last one. I arrived home happy for having had such a productive night and, of course, emotionally intelligent.

Chapter 11

It was just what was missing!

As Rose dialed the number, her heart raced with anticipation. She needed to share this news, and there was only one person she wanted to tell first.

Hello? Doctor Norma? (...) It's Rose... Are you doing well? (...) I'm calling to give you some good news. Since it's Saturday, I didn't want to wait until Monday... (...) No! No... ha! ha! ha! Percy remains distant and will be even more so now that the school year has ended. (...)

Yes! Yes... this was the last week of classes, and that's why I'm calling. I went today to check the exam results, and I just found out that I managed to complete high school. I wanted you to be the first to know. (...)

Of course, Doctor... in a way, largely, I owe this achievement to you. (...) I know... I know... there was my effort, determination, focus, blah, blah, blah... but, without comparing you to a farming machine because you are far too elegant, it was you who, like a tractor, constantly pushed me forward. You turned me into fertile ground and seeded me with a bunch of words like faith, hope, truth, self-awareness, and above all, friendship. That's why I'll be eternally grateful to you... (...)

What? Celebrate? (...) Hmm... have coffee at the mall? Why not? But I think I'd prefer a big ice cream,

Doctor... the kind you keep eating until your butt starts clapping... (...) Ah! Ah! Ah!

Seriously, Doctor... I love ice cream! Do you like it too? (...) Banana Split? Really? (...) No! I've heard of it, but I've never tried it, is it good? (...) What do you mean from your time? You talk as if you're from the time when dogs were tied up with sausages... Geez! You're quite spry, Doctor! (...)

Don't mention it; it's not a compliment... it's the truth. But I like the idea of the mall... when? (...) Yes, yes... today in the late afternoon! That's a good time! By the way, Doctor... I've been reading my notes that I made every time we talked... (...) What? Yes, notes... I always mentally took notes and then wrote them down at home. So, I came up with some questions I'd like to ask you. I would have done that on Monday when I go to work... but this idea of the mall fits perfectly. (...)

That's right! We can talk while we have... what's it called? Banana split? I want to try this thing! Let's see if it's as good as you're saying. (...) Why? Is it too big? (...) Doctor... when it comes to ice cream, especially with banana and a sprinkle of nuts, cashews, and peanuts, I could eat mine and whatever you can't handle of yours! Ah! Ah! Ah! (...) True! (...)

Okay, Doctor... see you there then. Oh, yes... where? Okay, at 4 by the escalator on the second floor... it'll be great! (...) Thank you... you too! See you there!

As it struck 3 o'clock, I took a nice shower and put on an outfit suitable for a mall outing... a girly style. This mall where I was meeting Doctor Norma is super fancy. I've been there a few times alone, and I always feel like I'm at a party I wasn't invited to. Lots of snooty people, exuding arrogance and carrying bags from designer stores. I never understood why these people are so concerned with just buying expensive clothes and brands! I mean, one of the good things we do in life, we do without clothes! Geez!

I arrived at the escalator on the second floor... but the doctor hadn't arrived yet. I stood there looking at the shop windows, dreaming of having enough money to buy everything I desired. Everything was beautiful, but all too... too expensive for my budget! In fact, I've spent my whole life thinking that money was the most important thing. Today I'm sure of it!

I stood in front of a shoe display, eyeing a wonderfully expensive pair of sneakers. It would take a good chunk of my salary! I walked a bit further and stopped at a display of baby products. Wow! Diapers with a hefty price tag! It's contradictory... you spend a lot on something your kid is going to fill with poop! Geez! Suddenly, a hand touched my shoulder...

Hi Rose... it was the doctor... Have you been waiting long? Hi Doctor Norma... I replied, hugging her... No, not at all... I just got here. Are you okay? Better now, Rose... she said smiling and taking me by the arm... Let's go! Those banana splits are waiting for us!

We walked towards the ice cream parlor that, she said, she already knew from other summers. We walked and talked, looking at the displays, commenting on the prices. She was, as always, dressed with care and elegance. I felt as if she were my mother, taking her little one for a stroll in the mall.

We arrived at the ice cream parlor and soon found a table. After ordering two banana splits, she told me, with just a hint of sadness, that it was in that ice cream parlor that she met her late husband. Although I was curious, I didn't want to ask questions, afraid of seeming indiscreet. But she ended up telling me herself that many years ago, she was alone having ice cream when he approached and asked, "Is this seat taken?" "No!" she replied... "You can take it!" She told me that he kept looking at her and she said, "I said it's unoccupied, you can take it!" "You didn't understand..." he said... "I want to sit here, with you! Can I?"

Rose... she continued... I simply couldn't resist that sharp, penetrating gaze... well, I was still a student, with not much experience. So, I said, trying to be casual, "Alright then... sit if you like!" And he liked it, Rose... she said with a smile from ear to ear... so much that a year later we were already married, can you believe it? They were wonderful years of good companionship... we just didn't have children, but it was purely by choice for both of us. Today I regret it... I should have had a child. Today he would be about your age. But Rose... you never told me about you, your family...

Before I could start talking about myself, the banana splits arrived. Wow, doctor... I said looking at that "canoe" full of banana and ice cream... this looks more like a float! Wow... I'm going to indulge here!

But Rose... she began wielding the spoon and taking a bit of ice cream... you were going to tell me... wow, this is so good! Tell you about myself? ...I asked... already somewhat hypnotized by the banana split... oh, yes! Well, doctor, I'm the only child of a wonderful mother and an absolutely absent father.

He left... I continued... when I was still little. My mother used to say that one day he went out in the morning to buy some French bread and never came back. Probably, according to my mother, who was quite a joker, always in a good mood, he might have gone to buy the bread directly in Paris. Unfortunately, she passed away when I was 17. She had a heart problem, poor thing! Wow, it was a blow for me, doctor...

I can imagine... she agreed... you said she was humorous? Yes... I confirmed... she loved to laugh and make others laugh. I never missed a chance to make a joke... for example, you couldn't ask a silly question to my mother, she always had an even sillier answer. Like... mom, do you want fried chicken? "Of course, I'm not going to eat it raw?" she would reply, laughing.

Doctor Norma, laughing, almost choked on the ice cream! We had an alarm clock... I continued... one day I dropped the alarm clock, and it shattered on the floor. So, I shouted to her in the kitchen: "Mom... the alarm clock fell and stopped!" And she replied: "Of course... what did you expect, for it to start walking?" It was always like that, with Mrs. Olivia... but the times, Doctor Norma, were tough... in fact, our cows weren't even thin... they were downright anemic!

I didn't even finish speaking because the doctor was already cackling. Oh, Rose... she said... you confirm the old saying that the apple never falls far from the tree. Mrs. Olivia must have been a lovely person, just like you are!

With those words from the doctor, I don't even need to say that I felt all puffed up.

But Rose... she continued... how did you manage? Alone, without a father or mother... Well, doctor... I replied... I had to go live with an aunt, my mother's sister, who lived in the countryside. But my uncle, her husband, said he couldn't afford my schooling, so to live with them, I had to stop studying and work and contribute to the household expenses. I also had two younger cousins.

It was a tough time for me, doctor... I continued speaking while having the ice cream... because I didn't get along with my uncle, who was demanding and annoying. After he passed away, I came back to São Paulo. My aunt was left alone with the children, living off her and her husband's retirement. She's doing okay... the kids have grown up and they also work. Every now and then, I visit her.

Rose... she began between one spoonful to another... you mentioned you had some questions to ask. Right, doctor... I said, digging into a piece of banana covered in ice cream... so, changing lines...

It's lanes, Rose... she corrected, laughing. Oh! right... I agreed... but why lanes, doctor? She wiped her lips with a napkin and explained to me that lanes because of the act of changing lanes when driving.

Good thing... I grimaced... I wouldn't know, I don't drive. No way! So, doctor... I said, opening my purse... I have some doubts about a few things. I even wrote them down on this paper so I wouldn't forget. By the way, before you arrived, I was looking at some shop windows and getting scared by the prices. At those moments, I get angry with myself for not having money to have the things

I want and desire. Should I be angry at money for not having it in abundance?

No, Rose... she replied... never be angry at money. Do you know why?

Money is your friend!

Money is and always will be a great friend, Rose... she said with some gravity. But why, doctor... I asked... some have plenty and others have nothing? Is money choosing its friends?

She chuckled at the sincerity of my question. Rose... she explained... you have to consider that everything that happens in our external world is a reflection of our inner world. Our relationship with money is no different!

But doctor... I countered... what about those people who barely have enough to eat at home, live poorly, don't have access to quality education and healthcare... for them, it's harder to live than for those who were born rich, right?

Yes, absolutely, dear... but what I want to show you is that there's a better way to see the world. You see... there are many people from poor families, born in slums, who still managed to face these challenges and achieved great results.

But being born with a silver spoon... I asked... makes life easier, doesn't it? Yes, of course... she replied promptly... but being born rich doesn't guarantee that you'll keep that wealth. Simply because you didn't handle money intelligently. Being born into a wealthy family is no guarantee of anything!

What do you mean, doctor... I asked... no guarantee of anything? Well, Rose... because there are people who are complacent in the comfort of wealth and don't bother to maintain it. For them, adversities are problems and never challenges. They shy away from confrontation and, unconsciously I would say, don't feel deserving of the rich condition. So, little by little, the money goes away and all that wealth, poof!

On the other hand, she continued without touching the banana split... there are people who have a growth mindset. For them, adversities are challenges to be faced. With these challenges, they feel stimulated to have more determination to achieve everything they desire. They believe they are capable, and they succeed!

Right, doctor... I countered... I believe that these people you mentioned who have a mindset to grow and prosper certainly had an education geared towards that. They were well-guided, right? Whereas people who didn't have proper education because they were born poor will be destined to fail. Isn't that so?

Exactly... she said, pushing the banana split as if already satisfied. I was finishing mine and already eyeing what was left of hers.

Look, Rose... you touched on an important point: education. People who were born into wealthy families and weren't educated to face challenges, tolerate frustrations, and have a growth mindset end up failing. Why? Because they probably lost family support and had to try to grow on their own. Since they weren't educated for it, they fail.

I wanted to ask something, but my banana split was too good!

There are stories... she continued excitedly with the explanation... of people who suddenly became rich. In the lottery, for example. If they didn't have a good education for prosperity, they won't have a good relationship with money and will quickly blow through the fortune they won.

Doctor... I think my relationship with money is the same as I had with this banana split. I've already finished it off! Ah! Ah! Ah!... she laughed... you're a character, Rose! If you are cool with it... she said, pushing her banana split towards me... take what's left of mine!

Am I cool, doctor?... I replied with a smile... gosh, I'd be a restroom cleaner at a bus station if the payment was in ice cream. But you were talking about education for prosperity... (she was still laughing).

So Rose... wow that was a good laugh... so, you see how proper education adjusts people's lives for the better. So much so that these individuals, who were privileged with conveniences and learned to face challenges constructively, can further double the wealth they received.

Because they made good deals, I suppose... I interjected, skewering a piece of banana with ice cream. Not just for their aptitude in business, Rose... she countered... but also, and mainly, because of the positive mental attitude, aimed at achieving dreams, reaching goals, and, above all, prosperity.

So, you mean, doctor... I asked, pulling her banana split towards me... someone born into a poor family, but properly educated, has a chance to succeed? To prosper? Of course, Rose... she responded... we're talking about...

Wealth for those born outside the golden cradle

With proper education, everyone can prosper. Rich or poor... remembering that people from humble origins may take a bit longer to achieve financial success. Much more than those from wealthier backgrounds, since they don't have to worry about survival.

I'm glad to hear that, doctor... I said... especially now with a mentor like you.

Thank you, Rose... she said smiling tenderly... compliments are always welcome. But to continue, to confirm what I said, some people aren't satisfied with their own reality and use that dissatisfaction as a driving force to change it for the better. Challenges, for them, are provocations that encourage improvement, and they don't give up easily.

Wow, I'd love to be like that... I said, scraping the last bits of ice cream from the "boat". Rose... she scolded me gently... don't say "I'd love to be." Say "I am!" Say it... "I am!" Now?... I asked. Yes... she insisted... always! Come on, say it! I felt a bit awkward, but I couldn't resist the doctor's intimidating gaze and sort of mumbled: I-I am! Again, Rose... she said... but say it firmly... **I am! I can change my reality for the better. Always!**

I looked firmly at her and repeated: **I am! I can change my reality for the better. Always!** That's right, Rose... repeat after me: **I am strong, and every day I'm getting better and better!** Come on... repeat it! I wiped my mouth with a napkin and repeated: **I am strong, and every day I'm getting better and better!** Say that every day, Rose... until you convince your subconscious of it.

Wow... she was about to put her hand on my head and shout, "Out! This body doesn't belong to you!" But I said nothing... far from me to hurt the doctor with my jokes.

Very good, Rose... she said contentedly... words have power! Always remember that! That's why we shouldn't judge or speak ill of wealthy people. On the contrary... we should be inspired by them. Poor, but optimistic people who love prosperity don't see themselves as victims of society but as protagonists of their own story. They're determined to make everything work out and don't give up until they succeed.

You know, doctor... from all you've said, I believe I've never been poor. Just without money. Being poor is a state of mind. Being without money is a temporary situation. Am I right?

Absolutely right, dear... she said, signaling to the waitress. She ordered two bottles of water. Wow! The water came at a good time because I was really thirsty... also, after one and a half banana splits, I think I could drink a whole water tank!

Unfortunately, Rose... she began again... the vast majority of poor people accept poverty as if it were an unchangeable reality. They believe money is no good and that it's the greatest evil in the world. These ideas generate conflicts in the subconscious, and they end up being perpetually unhappy.

In truth, Rose... any poor person would like to become rich! Because money solves a lot of things, solves problems, and, of course, increases the quality of life. But if these people, unconsciously, believe that money is the root of all evil, that money destroys character and doesn't bring happiness... they'll never achieve prosperity!

My ex-mother-in-law... I interrupted... used to say that the rich won't enter heaven. So, Rose... she continued... all these ideas against money create internal conflict. Because there aren't people who don't want to go to heaven, who don't want to have character, or who don't like being happy.

Doctor... I interrupted again... point out one of those people, and I'll point you to a corpse. Someone like that must have died, goodness!

Ha! Ha! Ha!... she laughed... people with financial problems, Rose, need to eliminate the misconceptions they have about money. They need to feel prosperous and deserving so they can attract prosperity to themselves.

Is it related to the Law of Attraction, doctor? That was another question I... Absolutely, dear... she replied... this law brings to you everything that vibrates at the same frequency as you. It has a name... quantum physics, which is a topic for another time.

Doctor... I asked... does the Law of Attraction select people vibrating in the correct frequency? Interesting question, Rose... she said, taking a sip of water... the Law of Attraction is blind, you know? It doesn't judge, it doesn't reason... if a person, good or bad, believes they deserve and are capable of great fortunes and doesn't give up on that, they will attract what they believe.

So, doctor... I interrupted... that's why there are so many "tough" people out there, throwing money left and right, financially prosperous but with the character of a gangster, right? Exactly, Rose... she replied... and money intensifies that in them. In truth, the lack of integrity was already present in that person before becoming rich or richer. Money just highlighted that bad nature. Conclusion: money doesn't change people, it only intensifies what was already in them.

Doctor, one question... does the Law of Attraction only attract prosperity? No, Rose... of course not! Want more water?

No, thank you, doctor... from the ice cream and water standpoint, I'm already more than prosperous! Ha! Ha! Ha!... she laughed, taking a sip of water. Look, Rose... she continued... the Law of Attraction doesn't just attract prosperity or good things. But if a person exudes falseness, self-interest, and lack of character, they end up attracting people of that kind into their lives. Thus, despite all the wealth, they also find a great existential void.

So, doctor... I interrupted... can we prosper through goodness, doing good, and attracting good people to us, right? Exactly, Rose... she said with a smile... I see you've understood. That's why it's important to pay attention to how you're vibrating... do this by observing your thoughts.

That's why, Rose... she continued... self-awareness is important, and thus, paying attention to how you relate to money and what you're actually attracting into your life with your thoughts.

You know, doctor... I said... I believe the only solution for people who can't achieve self-awareness on their own, know about the Law of Attraction, control their emotions, etc... etc... is the help of a professional, in other words, undergoing therapy. So, I ask: what about people who can't afford a therapist?

Rose... she explained... we therapists usually say that the money spent on therapy sessions isn't an expense, but an investment! Perhaps the best investment one can make in themselves!

Wow, doctor... I said somewhat daringly... I wouldn't know how to pay for everything you've already done for me. Maybe I'd have to sell both my kidneys... Rose, Rose... she replied with the tenderness of a mother... you, besides being an excellent collaborator in the office, are also a great friend. You, even if unconsciously, complete me by playing the role of a daughter I always wanted to have but didn't. All the therapy I do with you is on the house.

Ha! Ha! Ha!... I laughed heartily and contentedly, feeling as if Percy were proposing to me... thank you, doctor! I'm immensely happy that you think so. Indeed, I have a true mother in you. I'd love to repay you for all the good you've done for me...

Rose, dear... want to repay me? Prosper! Prosperity is abundance, and abundance is energy that circulates, that flows. So don't stand still... and don't let your money stand still either. Put it to work, invest, study what's best for you, and allow things to flow and not stay stagnant in your life. Help people whenever you can, be good always, sharing only good things with everyone, give hugs and smiles, say words of encouragement to everyone around you, praise someone whenever you can...

I remembered a painting I saw in her living room, filled with phrases like these.

Rose... by acting like this, money will always be present in your life. Don't feel sorry for spending it wisely. Look... there are infinite possibilities of how money and prosperity can help you. But it all depends on how you feel on your predominant thoughts, and, of course, most importantly: on your endless process of self-awareness!

She kept talking, and I became more and more fascinated. Feeling more and more prosperous and the owner of a full life. I confirmed that the person in front of me wasn't just a doctor, a therapist, an employer... she was indeed a great friend, almost a mother. An invaluable treasure that I would preserve as long as it existed...

Rose... she said, placing her hands on mine... I wish for you, more than prosperous, to be very happy and successful in your life. Someone once said that success is what you want, and happiness is liking what you've achieved. I think you won't have any problem with that!

Doctor... I said, my eyes already moist... success will come later, when I finish college and become a doctor like you. But if knowing you and enjoying your friendship means happiness, then I'm already happy... and you can't imagine how much!

She, looking at me, stood up, and I instinctively stood up too, and we ended that afternoon with the strongest hug I've ever given and received.

Doctor Norma and her final advice:

Happiness

• *There is no path to happiness. Happiness is the path.* Thich Nhat Hanh

• *To find joy in the joy of others is the secret of happiness.* Georges Bernanos

• *Do not seek happiness outside, but within yourself, otherwise you will never find it.* Epictetus

• *Happiness is not the absence of conflicts, but the ability to deal with them. A happy person doesn't have the best of everything. They make everything better.* Albert Einstein

• *Happiness does not depend on what we don't have, but on the good use we make of what we have.* Thomas Hardy

• *Success is getting what you want, and happiness is liking what you got.* Dale Carnegie

Words have power

• *Words are like coins: one may be worth many, and many not worth one.* Francisco de Quevedo

• *True words are not pleasant, and pleasant words are not true.* Lao Tzu

• *All our words will be useless if they do not come from the depths of the heart. Words that do not give light increase the darkness.* Mother Teresa of Calcutta

• *Words can have the lightness of the wind, but also the strength of the storm.* Victor Hugo

• *Be careful with your thoughts, thoughts generate words, words generate actions, actions generate habits, and habits shape personality.* Dr. Norma

For life

• *Obstacles are those things you see when you take your eyes off the goal.* Henry Ford

• *We never separate from those we love, for what we are is love.* Karina DeOliveira

• *We are not a drop in the ocean, but rather the entire ocean within that drop.* Rumi

• *We cannot see our reflection in boiling water, just as we cannot see the truth in a moment of anger. When the waters calm, clarity arrives.* Dr. Norma

• *Love is what remains for today, after a troubled yesterday.* Karina DeOliveira

Epilogue

Finally, we reach the end of another chapter but remember we haven't reached the end of the story. There are a lot of good things yet to happen, you just wait!

One cool thing that is already happening is the fact that I passed the entrance exam. Soon, I will be attending college for Psychology. Well, going to college is the realization of an old dream, which I achieved thanks to Doctor Norma, my boss, "poster mother" and, above all, after my mother, the best friend I've ever had in my entire life.

All her guidance and advice, which I recorded in this book, led me to be a much better person, determined and focused on my goals. Of course, I haven't lost that good-humored nerve that I inherited from my mother. In fact, it is like the Adam's apple... we inherit it and it stays with us forever.

Dr. Norma also, like the "mother" she has always been to me, passed on valuable teachings, emotions and values. I see this as if it were a legacy too, which I now pass on to you. But, as I said, I'm not going to stop here!

My work at the doctor's office will continue. Especially now at this, let's say, university stage (how chic!), we will continue our conversations. I, of course, as always, will be writing everything down for later, in the form of a nice-to-read text, and will be passing it on to you!

So, wait... we'll be together again soon! A tender Kiss!

Rosemary

About the Author

Karina De Oliveira, teacher, psychoanalyst, holistic therapist, graduated in Physical Education and Integrative Psychoanalysis, began her journey of self-knowledge and mental development during the pandemic.

She lives in Florida with her husband and two daughters. After starting his psychoanalysis course, she experienced some changes in her own behavior based on many studies including NLP (Neurolinguistic Programming), Hypnosis courses and its different approaches, became a Reiki Master, learned philosophies and practices of Chinese Medicine and yoga, Access Bars and Facelift Practitioner at Access Consciousness.

Certified and Licensed Professional & Spiritual Life Coach by Dardah Business School and created her own service and teaching method of mental development.

She has a YouTube and Instagram channel called ABH Portal Holístico. If you liked this work and want to know more about the author, follow her on social media.

Instagram   Youtube

www.ingramcontent.com/pod-product-compliance
Lightning Source LLC
Chambersburg PA
CBHW020337160726
47992CB00004B/1872